children's spaces
from zero to ten

Judith Wilson

photography by Debi Treloar

LONDON · NEW YORK

Designer **Pamela Daniels**
Senior editor **Annabel Morgan**
Location research **Kate Brunt**
Production **Susannah Straughan**
Art director **Gabriella Le Grazie**
Publishing director **Alison Starling**

Stylist **Judith Wilson**

First published in 2001.
This edition published in 2013
by Ryland Peters & Small
20–21 Jockey's Fields
London WC1R 4BW
and
519 Broadway
5th Floor
New York, NY 10012
www.rylandpeters.com

10 9 8 7 6 5 4 3 2 1

ISBN 978-1-84975-367-8

A CIP record for this book is available from the
British Library.

Library of Congress Cataloging-in-Publication
Data has been applied for.

Printed and bound in China.

contents

introduction

Kids get everywhere, whatever space they're given. Newly arrived, even the tiniest baby has enough equipment to rival a squaddie. And, from the minute a child becomes mobile, not a square inch of your precious home will be sacred. Children are noisy, exuberant and have stuff by the crateload. They may drive the style queens among us to the edge, yet without them home would be too pristine a place.

This book won't maintain your hard-won, carefully designed space at the expense of your kids' physical and creative freedom. It won't

teach you to stencil a teddy-bear border, either. Instead, there is plenty
of inspiration here from real families, with real kids, who amply prove
that children and great design can co-exist happily, without either party
having to compromise on style. Armed with practical surfaces and
effective storage systems, parents can reclaim communal living areas
within a matter of seconds at bedtime and enjoy being grown-ups
again. And your kids will appreciate a vibrant, stimulating environment
that is practical and relaxed too.

Whether you are adapting a sophisticated, child-free zone in preparation for the arrival of a first baby, or starting from scratch because your small children have just outgrown your current home, some serious thinking is required. Plan all the important practical aspects first, and the design and decoration will be a breeze. Your kids' needs may seem obvious, but their demands change with alarming speed. This is even more crucial with a new baby. Impossible as it may seem, that chubby infant kicking and cooing on a rug will all too soon demand a space and life of its own.

If your style is streamlined and modern, celebrate. A contemporary interior is perfect for kids: bold planes of colour and sleek surfaces make a marvellous backdrop for the inevitable jumble of toys, paintings and accessories. The rules are simple: things must be practical as well as good-looking, and children must be taught to respect what the whole family shares. Don't think that little ones are naturally inclined to dayglo colours and cute motifs. Credit them with good taste, involve your kids in planning their spaces, and give everyone (including yourself) licence for fun and a free rein.

A baby's first room needs tranquillity and comfort, for both infant and parents alike. Keep things simple with clear colours, quick-access storage and a great view from the cot. Sensory touches add magic; perhaps a wind chime or twinkling fairy lights.

rooms for babies

1

THIS PAGE AND OPPOSITE
In a baby girl's nursery, a
whitewashed antique cot
with a cut-out heart motif
sets the tone for a simple
yet pretty room. Pastel-
painted peg rails hung with
tiny dresses brighten white

walls. Painted pieces of
board with old-fashioned
wooden pegs attached make
possible an ever-changing
display of nostalgic pictures,
family snaps and paintings
– there will always be
something stimulating for

your baby to contemplate.
Open shelves (below) are
a convenient way to stack
baby clothes, but allocate
one alcove to each clothes
type to avoid muddles.

A baby needs little in the early days, though department stores might try to persuade you otherwise. Many infants don't even move into their own room until the age of three months or older, perfectly content to swing in a cradle at their parents' bedside. Nevertheless, a new arrival needs its own bedroom, for changing nappies/diapers, storing clothes and to house a nascent collection of toys. A small room is fine. It is cosy, and most toddlers would rather play in the family space downstairs than in a bedroom.

The main nursery basic is a cot/crib. Simple styles are both practical and chic. More enticing options than traditional varnished pine are beech or cherrywood cots (though they will cost more), white-painted wood, colourful melamine or decorative ironwork. An antique or retro-style cot can look beautiful in a pared-down room but, for peace of mind, check that its dimensions meet British Standards guides, or the US equivalent, and always buy a new mattress. A cot bed, with slatted sides that are removed as the baby grows up, is a sensible, cost-effective option. Pick the plainest style you can find.

Frilly, character-emblazoned bumpers and valances will spoil the look of a simple, contemporary nursery. A padded bumper is a good idea, because it protects restless little heads, but choose one in plain colours and with quilting, not frills. Cotton sheets and blankets and a comforting quilt are the other basics. When your baby is a year old, you can add a baby pillow and cot duvet.

Nursery manufacturers have become increasingly inventive in recent years, so blankets and sheets now come in every shade from pretty pastels to vibrant hues. It's fun to pick and choose between different co-ordinated ranges, or add a retro piece or two. Team a pink gingham sheet with a tangerine blanket, for example, or add a home-made Noddy pillowcase to perk up plain white linens. A large single motif on a blanket looks smarter than a tiny repeated design.

The nappy-changing area should be efficient and fuss-free. Resist the temptation to buy a specialist unit; it will soon be redundant. A chest of drawers at the correct height, with a plastic padded mat on top, can double as a changing area. Store all the essential kit – nappies, wipes and creams – in the drawers immediately below, hidden away from inquisitive toddler siblings. Alternatively, place them on a chunky MDF shelf above the chest but within arm's reach. If you have enough space, consider designing a custom-made unit. You will need alcoves for clothes, cotton wool, nappies and so on, with a discreet pull-out or pull-down changing surface. If the changing mat is going to be on permanent view, pick one of the trendier designs. Funky fake grass or cloud images have a distinct edge over teddy bears. Hang a mobile above the mat: kids' mail-order catalogues often feature abstract ones, like trendy clips from which you can hang postcards or photographs.

A low, comfortable armchair is a must for feeding. Get a loose cover made in a sturdy, washable fabric – bright denim, robust linen or towelling. If there's enough floor space, beanbags in jelly-bean colours or wipe-clean vinyl cubes are great for babies who are learning to sit up or crawl.

Keep the room looking modern with fuss-free window treatments. If you'd prefer little ones not to wake with the dawn chorus, use blackout lining. A roller blind, Roman blind or

THIS PAGE AND OPPOSITE
The double divan with surround on a tubular frame is ideal for a toddler who has outgrown a cot but is not yet ready for a bed. In this room, strong colour creates a bold contemporary mood – the walls in egg-yolk yellow, the purple drawer unit, the scarlet duvet and the lime chair are stimulating and jolly. Practical clothes storage includes a rack for dresses and shoes (opposite, below), while a painted chest of drawers doubles as a nappy-changing unit.

An attic room with sloping ceilings makes a cosy nursery. Take advantage of a skylight by placing the cot directly beneath the window, but don't forget a blackout blind to cut out glare. Toddler Scarlet's room proves that pink and white, the classic little girl's colour combination, can be fresh and pretty. White walls, a white cot and neutral carpeting provide the backdrop, while pale pink accessories add decorative accents.

wooden shutters are simple and neat; or, if you'd rather have curtains, bright or strong pastel plains, checks or children's motif fabrics make the best choices. If you choose the latter, go for classic children's characters; they look more stylish than today's garish and over-publicized images. Or look to the more exclusive fabric houses, which often carry whimsical, abstract kids' designs at reasonable prices.

Plain painted walls and an easy-care floor create the most restful environment for a baby. Choose colours that you like for the early years – babies don't form their tastes this young. White walls and a neutral floor are a perfect backdrop for colourful accessories. But if you (and your baby) need stimulation, paint one wall in a bold shade such as cherry red or swimming-pool turquoise. If you prefer pastels, stronger tones like lavender or duck-egg blue make the best background for primary-coloured toys. Try painting abstract shapes: stripes or giant dots look good. And don't forget the ceiling – babies spend hours on their backs.

Crouch down by the cot and experience your baby's-eye view, then give him or her moving stimuli. Can your baby see through the window and spy trees, or view clouds through a skylight? If not, change the position of the cot. String the ceiling with colourful Chinese lanterns, party bunting or paper mobiles. You don't have to cover the walls with pictures, but you and the baby need something to look at. Initiate a personal collection now: a framed baby handprint or informal black-and-white baby portraits are more arresting images than most conventional children's art.

Use imaginative lighting to add a creative dimension. If there is an overhead light, fit it with a dimmer switch, essential for checking on the baby at night. Plunder both adult and children's lighting departments for unusual options. As well as 'magic lantern' children's lamps, which splash the walls with gentle colour and movement, consider a lava lamp, strings of flower fairy lights, an illuminated globe or punched-metal lampshades that cast pretty patterns. Buy a packet of light-up stars for walls and ceiling, which will glow long after lights-out.

The simple, neutral look does not suit every parent and every baby. One way to customize a tiny boxroom – often the only space available for a new baby – is to douse it in colour. In baby Archie's bedroom, the walls are transformed with zany stripes, while the cot was chosen for its distinctive silhouette and zesty lime colour. To achieve a similar effect with stripes, paint walls in a strong base colour – hot pink was used here – then use masking tape to mark out stripes of varying widths. For simpler splashes of colour, paint blank artists' canvases in bold shades and hang them around the room.

BELOW LEFT **Not all babies have the luxury of their own room. Sliding doors partition off this cot from an open-plan loft.**

BELOW CENTRE **Plan storage carefully, then get a carpenter to build it to your specifications. This cupboard has a pull-out changing surface and custom-made box to hold wipes, plus shelves for nappies. It also acts as a divider between the baby's sleeping space and play area.**

BELOW RIGHT AND OPPOSITE **A cot in a corner of the parents' room can be individualized in small decorative ways, with baby photos or colourful bunting.**

You'll need more space for baby clothes than you might expect. Little vests and sleepsuits make quite a pile, then there are gifts of clothes waiting to be worn, as well as outgrown garments. A wardrobe isn't essential. Instead, choose a generous chest with plenty of drawers, which can be updated with a coat of paint or contemporary handles. A giant laundry basket is a must. Wicker baskets, zinc tubs or colourful plastic crates stacked on shelves or tucked beneath the cot will all make tidying easy.

Your baby's room needs to be no-nonsense, but it must be safe and cosy too. Anticipate the investigative crawling phase by keeping blind cords short, trailing cables clipped and plug covers on, with a high shelf for any out-of-bounds items, and bars or catches on the windows. If you have a wooden floor, add a rug for softness, or choose a good-quality wool carpet that cleans up well. Sisal and coir are too rough for soft, chubby little knees.

In the same way that you would in any room in the house, strive for the perfect ambience. Everyone should feel tranquil and calm in the nursery. You'll reap the reward of planning for simplicity: neither you nor your new baby knows quite yet what their favourite things will be.

Little girls adore pink, but they love baby blue, dreamy lilac and grass green too. Give your daughter a clear, pretty canvas onto which she can stamp her personality with favourite things, and organize it sensibly, so that it's easy for her to keep tidy.

rooms for girls

THIS PAGE AND OPPOSITE Converted from a hallway in the basement of a Victorian house, Cordelia's bedroom is a triumph of clever planning. The MDF bed is scaled down to fit the room's narrow proportions, yet still holds drawers beneath and a bookshelf at its foot. Behind the bedhead wall is a full-height cupboard. If a room needs more light and planning regulations permit, a new window adds novelty. At night, this one is shuttered with MDF discs. An all-white room needs a splash of bold colour. Choose a small area and work through the colour wheel as the years go by.

> 66 *I like the windows in my bedroom. They look like balloons!* 99
>
> CORDELIA, AGE 4

Most little girls love pretty things. But give your daughter a break from the classic, flowery bedroom and instead provide her with a fresh, contemporary take on the look. Crisp fondant colours or an all-white room create the perfect background against which little girls can display their special treasures. For tomboys, more muted shades and quirky, abstract patterns are appealing. Guard against reliving your own childhood fantasies on your daughter's territory. Just because you were denied shocking pink as a child doesn't mean that she'll want it now.

If you're unsure where to pitch the style of the room, look to your daughter for inspiration. Amazingly, even a three-year-old will have strong opinions, so talk to your little girl about her favourite colours. If she's still too small, observe the things she's naturally attracted to. Does she reach for pink frilly dresses or a brightly coloured T-shirt? What colours does she choose when painting? These little clues can provide you with an excellent decorative starting point. Keep the details flexible, so that you can chop and change as the years go by. Painted walls rather than wallpaper, display space for treasured accessories and classic furniture all make for a relaxed, easy bedroom. Stick to simple styles and a streamlined layout, and the room will look effortlessly fresh and modern.

When a toddler graduates from a cot to a bed, it provides a timely moment for reassessing the bedroom and making stylistic changes. Focus first on the hard-working furniture, choosing colours later. Basic pieces won't differ hugely from the baby years, but now a good bed becomes the central focus. Invest in the best mattress you can afford. Children may be light but they need firm support, and a good-quality mattress should last for ten years. Think long and hard about the style of bed you choose. Girls will go through myriad fads, from Barbie-doll fever at five to seriously sophisticated at ten. Work backwards. If a classic style with a contemporary twist is suitable for a pre-teen, it can be made appropriately childlike for the earlier years.

Select a distinctive frame to make the bed a focal point and save traditional divans for teenagers or spare bedrooms. Plain and simple reconditioned hospital beds look cosy for tiny children, especially when accessorized with a graphic animal-motif duvet or piled high with candy-coloured floral pillows for older girls. Self-assembly MDF sleigh beds are another versatile option. The high curved sides mean little ones can't fall out, and the ready-to-paint frame can be reinvented in bubblegum pink then powder blue followed by hot orange as girly crazes wax and wane. If you need only a headboard, be inventive and customize one. In place of a conventional curved bedhead, choose a more contemporary rectangular shape, with cut-out circles or hearts. Think fairyland, think woodland grotto, and create a headboard from picket fencing or gold-painted wood adorned with faux gemstones.

Canopied and four-poster beds, bunk beds or sleeping platforms prove irresistible to girls, as well as providing extra space for friends who are sleeping over. For an adult

THIS PAGE AND OPPOSITE
With its patterned pillows, white walls and white shutters, this five-year-old's bedroom strikes the right balance: it's pretty, yet not inappropriately reminiscent of a boudoir. Children adore whimsical touches, so scour junk shops for unusual buys. Here, the illumination includes teacup sconces (above left), a goose that lights up and a tiny dressmaker's dummy, while the bedside radio is a car (above right). Ready-to-paint MDF furniture (left) can be customized with simple motifs such as dots, hearts and pretty colours. If a little girl has a large room, a double bed can offer a comforting oasis.

squeezed halfway up a tiny ladder trying to make the bed, high-level options may be marginally less popular. But you can have great fun designing a special bed. A simple wood or tubular metal four-poster affords plenty of decorative potential and looks very contemporary. Frames can be draped with brightly coloured netting one year and home-made strings of shells the next or, for older girls, adorned with inexpensive, glittery sari silks. Or you could create a canopy with a plain mosquito net hand-sewn with fake flowers. A raised bed can usefully accommodate storage or a desk underneath, and for stylistic continuity can be custom-made in materials used elsewhere in the house. Plywood, painted MDF and galvanized steel are all practical options, and will be softened with colourful bed linen and teddies.

If the bed was chosen by you, let your daughter make some choices too. Gradually amass a varied selection of bed linen so that as she gets older bedmaking becomes creative rather than a chore. Snap up odd sheets or pillowcases in department-store sales or hunt down flowery retro eiderdowns at junk shops or jumble sales. In the same way that little girls love to pick and choose their dolls' clothes, they'll relish the chance to mix and

THIS PAGE AND OPPOSITE **With its funky materials – rubber floor, plywood bed and polypropylene chair – eight-year-old Lucy's bedroom also has the basics for a teenager's den. A series of plain, colourful surfaces creates a versatile canvas that can be dressed up with floral beanbags or kept simple for a tomboy. An entire wall covered in blackboard provides endless entertainment. A custom-made platform bed in painted MDF or plywood, as here, is not only a brilliant space-saver, but also creates a cosy, self-contained unit for a child.**

66 *I love my bed, because it's nice and cosy. I keep lots of my special things up here.* **99**

LUCY, AGE 8

match pretty pillowslips and duvet covers. Provided they are from a complementary palette, crisp checks, plains and florals mixed with white will look wonderful jumbled together on the bed. Extras such as an embroidered baby pillowslip, cosy travel blanket, or appliquéd top sheet make the final effect more individual. For a particularly modern bed, choose plain linens in several hot shades – perhaps a cerise pillowslip and duvet cover teamed with a lime bottom sheet. All white is no fun for a colour-conscious child, but, if that's what you favour, at least customize a white duvet cover with a satin appliqué or button trim.

The bed may be top priority, but storage comes a close second. Plan for, or with, your daughter by writing an exhaustive list of everything she needs to keep in her bedroom, from toys and clothes to decorative inessentials. You will need flexible storage to accommodate a child's eclectic store of possessions, which can range from masses of tiny toys to bigger items like a dolls' house. Not everything has to be put away at all times, but each item should have a home. It's simply not true that children are naturally messy. Most love to be tidy. It's up to you to provide sensible storage so clearing up is quick and easy.

Provided the room is large enough, the smartest and simplest storage option is to fit a run of cupboards with floor-to-ceiling, flush-fitting doors along one wall. Behind this façade you can provide a multitude of different-sized shelves, roomy enough to hold individual crates for small items yet deep enough for piles of sweaters and jeans, and including space for a hanging rail. Open shelves may seem a tempting option for finding toys at a glance, but closed doors are preferable.

At bedtime you want the room to be peaceful, without a child's favourite toys temptingly on view. Once cupboard doors have been shut it doesn't matter how messy things are inside.

THIS PAGE AND OPPOSITE
Girlish schemes need not be
flowery: pale sugared-almond
tones look equally feminine.
In this seven-year-old's attic
eyrie, eau-de-Nil walls, pastel
bedding and butterflies do the
trick. For a little girl who
values privacy, create a hideaway. String suspension wire
between walls to divide off the
bed area, and add a voile
curtain. 'Found' objects lend
romance: here, a cabinet is
home to an eclectic mix.

THIS PAGE AND OPPOSITE
Many little girls love a heady
mix of florals, and three-year-
old Cyprus is no exception.
Avoid floral patterns that are
too closely co-ordinated and
add splashes of a primary
colour, perhaps a scarlet
pillowslip, to give essential
bite to the sweeter pastels.
Combined with an iron
bedstead and painted wood
furniture in strong shades,
the look is fresh and modern
rather than traditionally
rustic. To focus attention on a
floral bed, play down the rest
of the decor, sticking to white
walls and plain curtains, and
add a variety of pillows and
cushions for a grown-up feel.

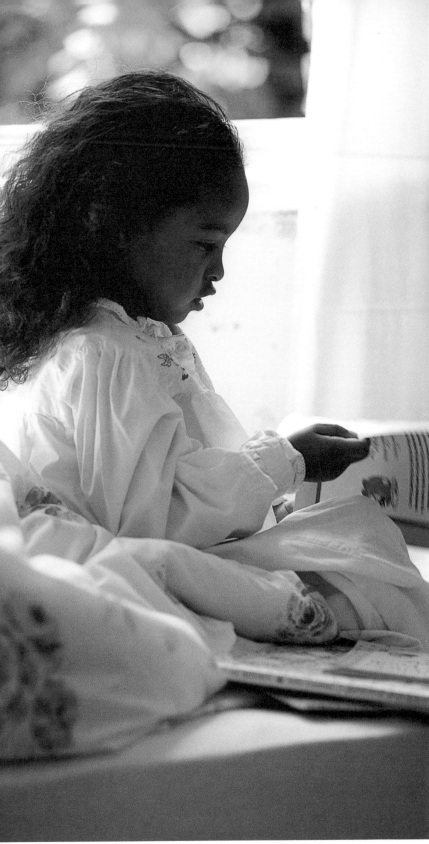

THIS PAGE AND OPPOSITE
A four-poster lends instant
glamour to a bedroom – perfect
for pre-teens. A simple metal
frame becomes dramatic and
sophisticated when swathed
with fabric – anything from
pastel voile to sari silk – that
has been hemmed and given
a slot heading. Alternatively,
try inexpensive shop-bought
tab-top curtains that can be
changed regularly. Choose
grown-up plain bed linen, in
white or bright plains. The rest
of the bed frame can be dressed
up with Chinese lanterns, faux
flowers or a twist of fairy lights.

In the same way that little girls love to choose their dolls' clothes, they will relish the chance to mix and match pillowslips and duvet covers.

The doors can be as simple or as imaginative as you like. Paint them the same colour as the wall and fit small handles positioned at child height, and they'll all but disappear. An eggshell finish provides an ideal surface on which to display artwork.

Alternatively, you could make doors from Perspex, aluminium or plywood for a contemporary spin. If you are saddled with a chest of drawers that's practical but unattractive, site it in an alcove and fit it with modern flush doors.

Ideally, you should provide an area for your little girl to draw and do her homework. Shop-bought dressing tables and desks are often frustratingly small and have fiddly detailing. Take a tip from contemporary interiors and provide her with a long, low worktop with wall-mounted shelves above. It could be painted MDF or covered in stainless steel or colourful laminate. Put the computer here; beneath the bench, fit crates on castors for toys or books, a second stool for a friend, even a cabinet with lots of shallow drawers for colouring pens and paper.

If you add a mirror, a worktop can also double as a dressing table and display space. It's important for display areas to be comfortably within a little one's reach, not high up on a shelf. Don't be controlling about what she wants to show off. You may not appreciate a collection of glittery nail polish and papier-mâché fruit, but beauty is in the eye of the beholder. She, in turn, will appreciate an arrangement of grown-up fresh flowers. Little bowls and baskets will keep hairclips, jewellery and nail-stickers in order.

Most children relish being in a colourful environment and will want to be involved in choosing favourite shades for decorating their bedrooms. Painted walls are much more versatile than childish patterned wallpaper and provide a cleaner, fresher background for the inevitable jumble of brightly coloured toys.

THIS PAGE AND OPPOSITE
Both boys and girls liked themed
bedrooms, and don't assume girls
will want a fairy grotto. This little
girl's room, with its seafaring
theme, has delighted her since
toddlerhood. Provided the painting
is professionally done, a full-scale
mural is the perfect antidote to
a nondescript bedroom. Keep
the images bold, and consider
incorporating a shaped bed. This
bed is imaginative, beautiful and
practical: it was custom-made
for the space, including storage
drawers below the steps.

THIS PAGE **In a fashion-conscious household with modern architectural detailing throughout, a child's room can still be cosy and fun. Here, lime walls, purple rubber flooring and a scarlet spotted bedcover and colour-blocked pillowslip are very appealing to little eyes.**

OPPOSITE **Junk shops are good places to find pieces of furniture for a toddler's room. Antique cots often come in non-standard sizes. Here, Jada's will do service until she is at least three.**

See what happens when you offer some paint colour charts to your little one. You may be amazed at her innate good taste and the shades she picks.

Older girls will enjoy dipping into sample pots and painting large squares of cardboard to prop up against the walls while deciding on a shade. Follow the same colour rules as you would anywhere else in the house. Jolly brights like sherbet yellow or cornflower blue are stimulating, but use them on a single wall so the effect isn't overpowering. If your daughter wants a pastel and you don't, shift the tone to an off-pastel for a more sophisticated effect. Or suggest positive alternatives: substitute lilac for pink, or soft leafy green for the more usual pale yellow.

If you're set on a contemporary style and your daughter wants an ultra-feminine retreat, try to find a compromise. An exuberant flowery fabric will please you both, provided it is tailored into a Roman blind instead of full curtains and teamed with a simple aluminium bed frame and plain sheets. Or keep walls and windows simple, with white paint and white self-patterned voile, but choose floral bed linen. Butterfly or leaf motifs are good alternatives to hearts and flowers, or you can achieve a girly look by customizing a white blind with sequins and covering large floor cushions in shell or eau-de-Nil satin.

If you simply can't agree, and want to avoid making expensive mistakes, fit the window with a plain roller blind, simple metal pole and curtain clips. Style-conscious little girls can then ring the curtain changes with anything from a length of Liberty Tana lawn to spotty voile. Cover the nursery armchair in cheap, washable white cotton duck and make cushions together. Citrus-coloured linens with a bright monogram or pink denim with purple cross-stitch will look trendy and smart.

Every little girl needs a space to display her artwork, poems or photographs. Conventional cork or padded pinboards are often too small. Much smarter is a large piece of steel, powder-coated in a shade to match the walls. Use magnets to attach drawings, cards and pictures, allowing displays to be changed frequently without stripping the paint from the walls. Glass clip-frames or painted wood frames arranged symmetrically are a smart way to display photos or to create an informal family tree. Imaginatively framed school artwork, with a bright mount, can turn a naïve illustration into stunning Pop Art.

Remember that, good as you want your daughter's room to look, it is her own private haven, a place for chats with friends, somewhere quiet to do homework, a retreat for dreaming and scheming. Providing privacy for children is vital. Help your daughter to mark out her own territory so that she can be alone when she chooses. You could adorn her door with a giant gilded initial or get a metalwork company to cut out her name in stainless-steel letters. Alternatively, she might enjoy hand-painting her monogram using special calligraphy. Try to agree on a more imaginative sign than a hand-scrawled 'Keep Out'. A necklace strung with colourful lettered beads and hung over the door handle is far prettier. Use ingenuity to provide her with a cubbyhole for secret things. If replastering is on the agenda, could a small alcove be inset into the wall? Perhaps a tiny built-in cupboard could be set into a boarded-up fireplace?

Bedrooms should be fun, so indulge in a smattering of kitsch. Search out funky extras: a beaded curtain to hang over the doorway, a glitterball to spin from the ceiling, a leopard-print cushion. Most mothers are little girls at heart. If you like something, the chances are that your daughter will too.

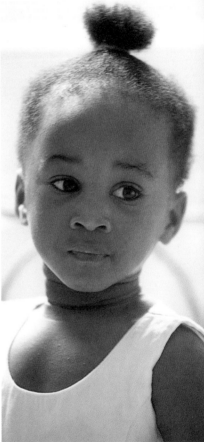

rooms for boys

For boys, create a cool den that's fuss-free and has versatile furniture for imaginative play. Raid the colour spectrum for inspiration – scarlet, leaf-green, indigo – then team a choice of bright colours with robust surfaces like rubber and wood, so no one worries about the inevitable scrapes and dents.

3

Very small boys need a tranquil atmosphere and tactile textures to promote a safe, cosy feel. In two-year-old Flinn's bedroom, a high picket-fence headboard, faux-fur rug and thick curtains do the trick. In a room with lots of natural daylight, heavy interlined curtains will cut out glare. Storage is not only practical but also lots of fun: a bookshelf loaded with colourful books (below left) and a collection of little shoes piled high (below centre) create plenty of contrast with the peaceful white walls.

Boys care passionately about their bedrooms. From around five years old, most know instinctively what accessories and motifs are 'cool' and will want to incorporate at least some into their private space. They may fuss less than girls about an overall scheme, but are obsessive when it comes to the smaller details. What boys need most is empty floor space – as much as you can spare – and plenty of storage so that their myriad collections, from toy soldiers to racing cars, can stay sorted and ready for play. Furniture that offers a bit of action – ladders to climb, platforms to scoot along – goes down a storm, too.

Rule number one is that everything in a boy's room should be robust. When play becomes rowdy, he won't think twice about bashing the bedhead. If you plan for this eventuality, everyone can relax. For example, a wall-mounted, enamel-shaded bedside lamp is a more sensible option than a fragile Japanese paper one, and a sturdy metal sports locker is more practical than a canvas beach-hut wardrobe. Imagine each piece of furniture being jumped off, climbed on or moved around as part of a pirate-ship game or impromptu kickabout, and you'll get a realistic picture.

Little boys need efficient, well-planned storage to help to keep their things in order. For toys, the ideal storage system combines plenty of small drawers, crates or boxes for compartmentalizing tiny toys with bookshelves and perhaps taller storage space for larger items.

LEFT **If space is tight, then choose a single, all-purpose piece of furniture, with drawers for clothes, shelves for books and a spacious top that can double as a display area for treasured possessions. Coats and shirts are easily hung on wall hooks. The bedroom is the ideal place to display a child's artwork, so hang a giant pinboard on one wall.**

" *I like my room because it's clean and tidy.* "

With this in mind, it makes sense to pick tough, scratch-resistant modern materials like laminate and plywood, or painted furniture that can be easily touched up with a new coat of paint.

In a boy's room too, the bed is bound to be the central focus. In acknowledging that fact, why not be bold and situate it in the middle of the room: a bunk bed can be more readily turned into an imaginary ship or climbing frame if it's easy to get at.

In terms of changing tastes and needs, boys have a steeper developmental curve than girls. They still require a cosy sleeping nook at the age of three, but by five they are ready for a more adventurous, classically boyish option. There are various options for tackling this challenge. Either buy a generously sized cot bed for the baby stage, and get a serious boy's bed once your son outgrows the cot. Or invest in a grown-up bed when he reaches the age of two, and make it inviting with a jolly duvet and accessories for the early years. A bunk bed is an excellent option. Your son can sleep on the safe lower level until about the age of six, and graduate to the higher level when he feels ready.

Boys, as much as girls, appreciate a fuss being made over their beds. Not only somewhere to sleep, the bed also represents a special safe and secure zone, as well as being a potential platform for imaginative games. Ready-to-buy modern options might include sophisticated dark wood or painted bateaux lits or sleigh-bed frames, simple iron bedsteads, colourful melamine platform beds with storage drawers, and sturdy tubular metal and canvas army-camp styles.

You will achieve the most individual results by dreaming up a customized bed. In an attic, a built-in MDF bed can be slotted in beneath sloping eaves, with roomy pull-out drawers beneath, all faced in tongue-and-groove. For an older boy, a simple plywood platform becomes something special when supported on giant castors or tubular metal legs. Alternatively, you could commission a carpenter to build a boat or a spaceship pod around a standard divan. A theme bed can look stunning, provided the rest of the decoration in the room is simple and clean-lined.

OPPOSITE **A treasured collection of colourful Ladybird classics bring a splash of colour to Flinn's snug bedroom.**

BELOW **A child-size washbasin, perhaps a small cloakroom model, is a boon in the bedroom – great for encouraging teeth-brushing. Cross-head taps/faucets are the easiest for little fingers to turn. This is also an ideal spot to site a medicine cabinet to hold child-related basics, but hang it high on the wall and make sure that it is securely lockable.**

THIS PAGE **Instead of traditional sludgy shades, choose quirky, vibrant colours for a trendy, bright boy's room like this one belonging to eight-year-old Gabriel. Floorboards can be coated in a tough, glossy floor paint for a practical finish. In a small room, a bunk bed (even if the child doesn't share) is a great idea, acting as a chill-out area and climbing frame as well as a sleepover space for friends. A custom-made desk is more fun than a traditional design. Wall-mount as much furniture as possible, leaving space for all the essentials of the boy zone – a football table, punchbag, dartboard or basketball hoop.**

For most boys older than five, a bunk bed or raised sleeping platform is a dream option. These days, many shops stock tubular metal bunk beds, which are more stylish than the pine variety. If you'd prefer to build a platform bed, various modern materials such as stainless steel, plywood and painted MDF are all good options. Think about safety and access. There should be a guard rail along the open side of the bed – one that a little body can't wriggle through in the middle of a dream. For access, a ladder is the most conventional choice, but make sure it's fixed securely in place. Metal rungs firmly attached to the wall beside the bed also look good. If there's room, a staircase created from giant building blocks is an imaginative way up to bed. Boys appreciate little extras, including mini-slides, rope ladders and clip-on ramps (perfect to join up two bunk beds if boys are sharing). Tie-on canvas or sailcloth panels are also good for imaginative play.

Since a raised bed frees up more floor space for play, it is a particular boon in a small room. Storage cupboards, a generous length of worktop or, in the case of a lower bed, lots of pull-out drawers, can be variously incorporated underneath. Whatever bed you choose, when planning the remaining bedroom furniture try to find streamlined pieces that don't encroach on valuable floor space, or movable items that can be pushed up against the wall during energetic games. Make furniture on castors a theme – everything from a chest of drawers to a low play table. Even better, make it easier to keep the floor clear by installing wall-mounted shelves for books, baskets for bits and pieces, hooks for clothes and even ceiling-suspended seating – perhaps a hammock or a swinging pod chair.

" I like my bed because I can sleep on the top bunk. Sometimes a friend stays the night and sleeps underneath. The colours are great because they really make my room stand out. "

GABRIEL, AGE 8

Little boys need efficient, well-planned storage so that their things can be kept in order. Most boys have minimal interest in clothes and in putting them away, so devise a simple storage system. Open shelves in a cupboard are the easiest option, but label each section for T-shirts, jeans and so on. Alternatively, build a series of box-shaped cupboards at child height all around the room, with each one devoted to a certain category of clothing, and fitted with a different-coloured MDF or stainless-steel door to resemble a sports locker. The top of the cupboards can be used for sports trophies or toy display. A hanging rail isn't a priority. Instead, give your son a long row of child-height hooks where he can hang up his pyjamas or anything else that has been strewn across the floor. Don't expect him to line up his boots and shoes neatly. Instead, provide one big basket, and agree that this is the designated place for all shoes at tidy-up time.

The older a child gets, the more time he'll spend playing in his room. For toys, the ideal storage system combines plenty of small

crates or boxes for compartmentalizing little things (cars, Lego, plastic animals), bookshelves, and perhaps taller storage spaces for larger items like a pop-up tent or sports equipment. Settling down to play is much less enticing if toys are in a muddle, and most children are appreciative of a freshly sorted-out bedroom. A simple wood or melamine unit, with alcoves for slotting in toy crates, is a very sensible option, and looks cool and modern when fitted with crates painted in a rainbow of funky colours. If you have the budget, look in contemporary furniture stores for Dayglo polypropylene pieces – drawer units on castors, for example, or folding tables – all of which provide trendy, versatile storage that will grow with your child. If space is in short supply, giant shallow boxes on wheels can be built to slide under the bed, though they should be fitted with plenty of dividers.

Indulge your little boy's passion for complex structures, be they intricate Lego structures or an elaborate toy fort or castle, and make sure that you give him a proper surface for displaying them.

BELOW **Some boys like their bedrooms to be uncluttered and no-nonsense. Brighten up the army-camp look with a few outrageous touches. The giant Stars and Stripes and the faux-ponyskin cushion make this room as cool as a teenager's den.**

THIS PAGE AND OPPOSITE
Brilliant, saturated colour on every surface, from walls to furniture, turns an ordinary bedroom into an entertaining playroom, usually the best option if a boy has a large, sunny room. Don't stop with the walls: paint skirting boards, cupboard doors, the bed and bookcase, all in vivid Smartie shades. Dark floorboards will balance the strong colour, while a cotton rug makes for comfortable floor play. In this five-year-old's room, the startling walls are matched by equally vibrant bed linen – a riot of crazy stripes, animals and exotic fruits.

Give your little boy a display area that can be devoted
to treasures such as christening gifts, home-made models
and toy cars. A thick MDF shelf fixed above the bed and
painted in a bold colour is a great choice.

THIS PAGE AND OPPOSITE
**Detailing counts for just as much
in a child's bedroom as it does in
a grown-up space. Ornaments
should be colourful and fun,
though many children do like to
display more formal christening
gifts. Give boys plenty of space
to show off their funny papier-
mâché creations and treasures.
A shelf unit (below) can be the
centrepiece of a room. It needn't
always be immaculately tidy:
you'll learn to appreciate the
innate, chaotic charm of kids'
mess! Children love anything that
spells out their name. Letters on
the door (opposite, below) lend
an air of importance, as does
anything monogrammed.**

The floor is not the best place for a little boy's display space
because special treasures will have to be removed for floor-
cleaning. Instead, provide a low table and tell everyone that this
is no-go territory. Cover the tabletop in something indestructible,
like stainless steel or oilcloth, so that it doesn't matter if there are
glue spills or paint splodges while craft-making is in progress.

In addition, little boys need a desk or computer table for
working at, complete with task lighting and a good chair: there
are plenty of groovy swivel seats in the shops. Also give him a
display area that can be devoted to treasures such as christening
gifts, home-made models and toy cars. A thick MDF shelf fixed
above the bed, perhaps painted in a bold colour, or a stainless-
steel catering rack for older boys, is a great choice.

Little boys play constantly on the floor, so flooring should be hard-wearing and attractive as well as providing a smooth surface. There's nothing more frustrating than trying to race cars along badly sanded wooden boards, or to arrange army platoons on bumpy sisal matting. Far more practical, and infinitely smarter, are painted or waxed wooden boards, smooth wood-laminate flooring or brightly coloured rubber tiles. Wooden boards needn't be left their natural colour: they could be graphically painted with roads, grass verges and rooftops for a car fanatic, or in startling purple gloss with yellow planets for a space fan.

Boys appreciate comfort, however, so add a thick, cosy rug as well. You could choose a grown-up abstract design in jolly colours that the kids will appreciate too. Some children's mail-order catalogues stock dual-purpose rugs with snakes and ladders or hopscotch designs, which can be both played with and sat on. A rug could even be the starting point for a simple decorative theme: a zebra print inspiring a Jungle Book mood complete with a fake leopard throw on the bed, or a groovy fake-grass rug for a tractor and farmyard fanatic.

THIS PAGE **This toddler's bedroom
has been created from a sectioned-
off area of loft. The plywood
storage unit acts as a divider
between the room and the living
space. Tall ceilings can feel
impersonal, but by enclosing the
bed with high sides, a cosy corner
has been created for a little boy.**

OPPOSITE **Kids adore sleeping in
nooks and crannies, so don't turn
the space beneath the eaves into a
wardrobe. A built-in bed might be
more fun. Work with the shapes
you have. Here, a bookcase is part
of the design, but the space it
occupies could equally be used
to create a secret cupboard.**

Although they respond instinctively to colour and pattern, little chaps generally show less interest than girls when asked to select a favourite paint shade or decorative theme. Don't force them. Instead, whitewash the walls and inject splashes of contemporary colour – anything from a broad-striped scarlet and white duvet cover to a giant orange felt pinboard or lime and indigo denim beanbags. They'll soon tell you if the don't like the colours.

If plain walls are too boring, there are plenty of quirky ways to decorate. One wall draped from floor to ceiling with a giant flag looks bold and stylish. Alternatively, line the walls with colourful maps, fit a floor-to-ceiling blackboard for boys to scrawl on, or use a metallic-silver wallpaper (great as a background for space paintings). Carefully chosen, large props mounted on the wall will also look modern against a single bright colour. What about a boogie board, a giant fishing net threaded with plastic fish, or a series of large plastic dinosaurs creeping across the ceiling?

If your little one is mad about a cartoon character, whether it be Bob the Builder or Batman, indulge his passion with a single giant floor cushion made up in appropriate fabric, or an enormous poster, then ignore further demands. Crazes come and go, and next year your little boy will have moved on to another phase. A generic theme, subtly done, is much more enduring and gives you a strong decorative 'hook' as a starting point.

If you create a neutral canvas with plain painted walls and a white roller blind, you'll have the freedom to introduce all manner of different themes. Kitted out with a green rubber floor, cowhide-patterned furniture and a blue ceiling, the bedroom becomes a farmyard retreat. With timber decking, porthole-shaped windows and a boat-print duvet cover, he'll be exploring at sea every night. Whatever theme you choose, ensure the key elements are inexpensive and easy to change.

THIS PAGE AND OPPOSITE
**A platform bed is a marvellous
space-saver in a narrow room. In
this seven-year-old's bedroom,
raising the bed off the ground has
freed up the floor area for play,
and created space for cupboards
either side of the doorway (above
right). The bookcases are wall-
hung so as not to impede play
space. This room shows how
to reinterpret the classic boys'
theme – boats – without covering
everything in motifs. With its
decking-effect beech boards and
metal bed rail, a yacht springs
instantly to mind.**

Boys may be boisterous and busy, but there are times when
they want a special area in their bedroom for relaxing and being
with friends. If there's no space in your little boy's room for a
sofa, give him the chance to turn his bed into a lounge-lizard
spot. He will enjoy touchy-feely fabrics on the bed. Keep duvet
covers and sheets in strong plains (T-shirt jersey bedding is a
good texture) and add a pure wool checked blanket. A giant
fleece-fabric blanket in a vivid hue such as scarlet or grass green
looks neat tucked over the duvet by day. A cut-up old sleeping
bag made into squishy cushions is also fun.

Give boys the chance to create their own ambience in the room
using interesting lighting. A bubble lamp by the bed, a light-up
globe on the desk or a funky coil of lights are all good options. Try
to squeeze in a few quirky additions. A football table, punchbag
or wall-hung basketball hoop will make your son's room the
coolest den he could ask for.

" I love climbing up the ladder to go to bed. It's a special place up there. "

CHRISTY, AGE 7

shared rooms

Siblings sharing a room need clearly marked personal zones, their own private corners and decorations that they both adore. If there are two of them, kit out their room with two of everything, then create a fun environment that's ideal for shared play, yet serene enough for soothing bedtimes.

4

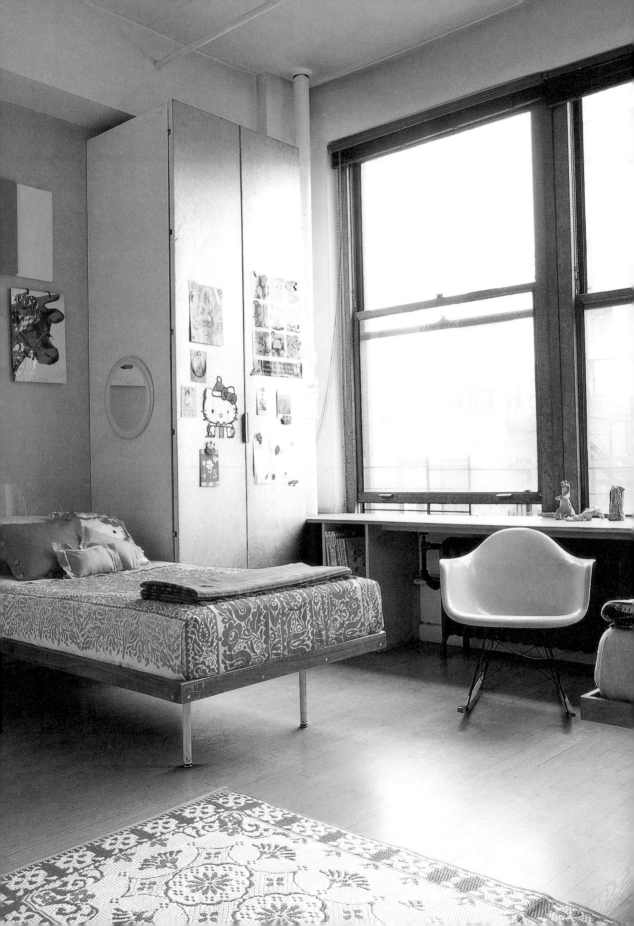

Plenty of children share a bedroom. As a parent, you may anticipate only the downsides: disrupted bedtimes, arguments over territory, one child wanting to study while the other chooses to chat. But it needn't be a nightmare. Ask any grown-up who shared a room to recall childhood memories, and many will fondly remember the fun of reading by torchlight after lights-out or the pleasure of two sets of toys. Besides, for a child to wake up with his siblings and fall asleep with them each night is a great gift. Approach decorating a shared bedroom with confidence, and the results will be fun for everyone. Younger siblings may even be fighting to squeeze in.

Demarcation of territory is crucially important. From an early age, children love to have personal space where they can keep their special treasures and retreat with toys or friends. If your kids are small, it's your job to decide who has what space, but include older children in the conversation. Start with a floor plan and move around scaled-down cut-out pieces of furniture that need to be incorporated to see what works well. If the room has great proportions and two windows, the most sensible option is to split it down the middle. It's more likely that allocating the space will include some compromises, and divisions may not be exactly equal in terms of area. Try to compensate fairly. If one child gets the window, give the other the mantelpiece for display.

Kids will find it fun (and you will find it politic) to have a formal division of territory, so that during arguments or when entertaining friends each can retreat to their private zone. First, decide if the division will be visual or physical. For little ones, the less physical separation the better. They will derive comfort at night by having their beds close together, and reading a joint story will be simpler for you. It might be amusing to divide the room with a brightly painted line of coloured footprints or chunky

THIS PAGE AND OPPOSITE **One way to approach a boy-plus-girl shared room is to keep the basics unisex. In this room, shared by a three-year-old girl and seven-year-old boy, polished boards, metal cupboards and identical beds provide a neutral backdrop. Give each child's area a distinct character of its own by using the bed and wall behind it as a focal point. Paint it in hot pinks and oranges for a girl and in muted tones for a boy. And consider the layout: would the kids prefer to sleep at opposite ends of the room or side by side?**

An individual wall display beside each child's bed is a good way to delineate territory. Here, boldly coloured walls are a stunning background for an assortment of objects – tiny dolls' clothes, pictures, photographs and other treasures. Retro furniture is ideal for kids' rooms. If a piece is not in pristine condition, it doesn't matter if it gets the odd knock, and furniture may come in wild colours with practical wipe-clean laminate surfaces.

arrows on the wall or a wooden floor. Older siblings will relish imaginative solutions that section off the bedroom. Consider a plasterboard wall with cut-out portholes so the kids can still chat to each other, or a floor-to-ceiling sliding MDF screen. Boys might enjoy individual custom-made screens in hole-punched steel that they can wheel to the end of the bed; girls could have four-poster beds draped with voile or organza for privacy.

If your children get on well, divide up the room space into sleeping, play and work zones instead of two distinct areas with bed, chest and so on. This is the most sensible option for older children or if space is restricted. Bunk beds or sleeping pods on a shared platform can be separated from the play space with a sliding screen or floor-to-ceiling sheer curtains. The children can either share one long countertop to do their homework, or have two identical desks side by side.

If older children find it hard to concentrate with two of them in the room, put up a plywood screen between them, which can

double as a pinboard. The remaining floor area can be devoted to fun and games, and there's no further need for a playroom.

When a boy and a girl share a bedroom, your most pressing problem is likely to be how to reconcile two definite and probably wildly differing tastes. In the case of very young children, one solution is to paint the walls white or in a bold single shade, then concentrate on personalizing each child's bed.

There's nothing more charming than two identical bedsteads side by side, but give each of the beds a distinctive character by using different duvet covers – an identical design, perhaps, but in two contrasting colours. You can take the theme a step further, and colour co-ordinate each child's bedside table, rug and lampshade. If your children occupy a shared bunk, individuality is even more essential. Personalize each level of the bunk with favourite toys and cosy cushions. Alternatively, you can keep the look co-ordinated by choosing differently patterned duvets but in toning shades.

When it comes to wall colour, older siblings will have fun poring over paint charts to find a hue that both can agree on. Provided shades are tonally harmonious, the most extraordinary combinations can work, and the look will still be confident and modern. For a cohesive scheme, select three shades. Use one for the girl's bedhead wall and another for the boy's bedhead wall. A neutral shade works well with brights, so, if your daughter wants shocking pink and your son is into army fatigues, give the boy a strong khaki. The third shade can be introduced in the form of upholstery on one side of the room and picture mounts on the other. Bringing together such a mixture of contrasting hues sounds outrageous, but combined with white duvets and a wooden floor it can look fabulous.

Kids' varied tastes in pattern are harder to resolve. A safe bet is to stick to checks, stripes or spots, but if little girls want something floral, an abstract flower-print duvet cover will sit well with, for example, a boy's car silhouette. Alternatively, a colourful fantasy mural will appeal to both sexes, but try to keep shapes simple and the look graphic.

66 *I love my room because it has my name all over the place. And I love the bookshelf. Now I don't have to keep my books under the bed.* **99**

GEORGIA, AGE 6

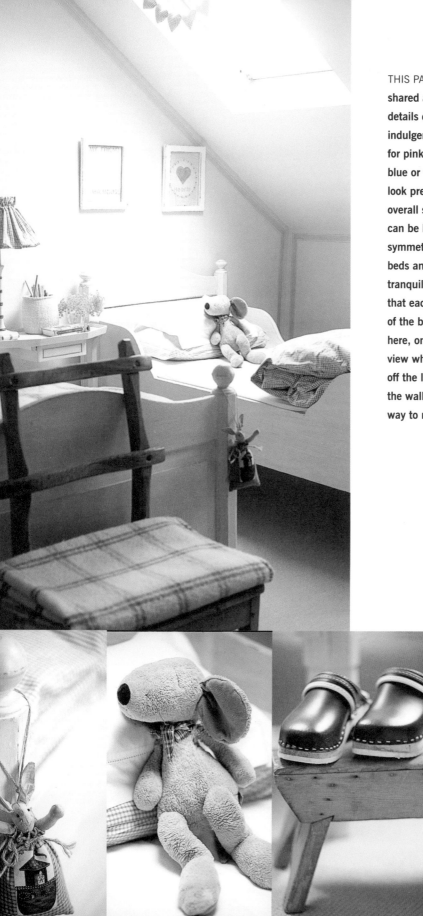

THIS PAGE AND OPPOSITE **In a shared all-girls room, decorative details can be a little more indulgent. Both girls may clamour for pink, but cooler shades, soft blue or faded red perhaps, still look pretty. If both girls love the overall scheme, most elements can be kept identical. Here, the symmetry of side-by-side sleigh beds and twin chairs creates a tranquil ambience. Make sure that each child has her fair share of the best elements of the room: here, one child has the skylight view while the other gets to turn off the lamp. Wooden letters on the wall (opposite) are a subtle way to mark out boundaries.**

THIS PAGE AND OPPOSITE
One neat way to sidestep the issue of children with differing tastes is to install a fabulous mural that will dominate their bedroom. Somehow a mural negates the need for boundaries, because the room becomes a separate entity, everyone's room, a magical place to go to sleep and wake up in. A mural is also a good way to disguise awkward dimensions: in Millie, Florence and Isabel's bedroom, the tree shape was inspired by the chimney breast. The mural will inject an element of fantasy. Who cares about sharing a shelf when everyone can stack books on a tree branch?

Cool pastels teamed with boldly coloured checks and stripes make the perfect combination if a girl and boy share. The girl's bed can be dressed up with flowers, and the other made more boyish with darker sheets and pillowcases.

If you are considering adding a mural to your children's bedroom, remember that generic themes usually make the best choices because they won't date too quickly. Properly painted, a woodland grotto, summer sky or moonscape can transform a plain bedroom. Kids adore tiny details. Two giant green leaves painted on a white wall and crowded with red and black aphids will keep them amused for many bedtimes. The remaining details should be kept simple. Plain, understated window treatments and duvets, simple bedsteads and contemporary wood or rubber flooring will take the edge off an excessively cute visual appeal.

Think how you might incorporate imaginative lighting into your children's bedroom mural. Twinkling wall lights emerging from a faux boat mast or starry sky are quite magical for little kids on the brink of sleep.

When same-sex siblings are sharing, you can easily indulge all-girl fantasies or all-boy passions. But you still need to personalize the two-of-everything accessories, so that sharers are clear about who owns what. You might want to keep the theme subtle with colour-coding: pink for one child's furniture and toy boxes, green for the other's. Bedding, laundry bags, lampshades and loose-covered chairs can all be individualized with a giant monogram, or allot each child a motif – perhaps a car for one, a butterfly for the other – which each can easily recognize as his or her own. Individual display areas, for everything from stones from the beach to photographs or framed certificates, and a section of wall or pinboard for personal artwork, are essential.

Some children are messy, while others are pin-neat, so, to avoid arguments over tidying, give each child his or her own chest of drawers, shelves or wardrobe. A bedside table for each, to hold a night-time drink, books and lamp, is also essential. Don't attempt to separate toy storage: if children are sharing a

" My sister Sophie and I talk after lights-out and plot midnight feasts. "

JACK, AGE 7

THIS PAGE **Two divans set at right angles, with a shared cube side table, is a comforting and sensible option for little children. Molly and Eli are in no danger of knocking over furniture, and** they can chat in bed while retaining a little privacy. In a shared room, good storage is essential, so consider below-bed toy drawers and low divans that can double as a daytime sofa.

ABOVE **Sharing a bedroom
is about fun, so it's a sound
investment to custom-build a
giant platform that can sleep
two or support one mattress
with a play area at the other end.**

bedroom, it makes sense for toys to be communal. It's a good
idea to provide a few lidded crates for each child, however, so
special treasures can be kept well out of the way of inquisitive
small siblings and their sticky fingers

Since shared bedrooms often double as playrooms, aim to
ensure that everything can be tidied away quickly and hidden
behind closed doors. Bedtime with two excitable children is
stressful enough without a jumble of tempting toys peeping
out from wicker baskets.

If you've picked a stimulating decorative scheme, installing
flexible lighting is one way to calm things down at bedtime. In
shared rooms, the correct level of lighting becomes even more
important. Different-aged children may have staggered lights-out
times, so that, while an older child needs a well-shaded task light
for reading in bed, his younger sibling might require a glowing
nightlight. For playtime, low-voltage ceiling lights give brighter
illumination than a single overhead pendant, but have a dimmer
switch put in so you can reduce the level of light at night-time.
Consider a wacky lighting feature that both kids will enjoy. For
example, either a giant clock light-projected onto the wall or an
illuminated fish tank would look stunning.

When children enjoy sharing a bedroom, it becomes a real den, their own private space versus the family house, and a brilliant place to chill out. If space permits, give them a daybed, a child-size chaise longue or an inflatable chair to lounge on, and consider installing a television for older kids. If there is a younger sibling who doesn't share, and everyone is in agreement, the daybed (or a put-up bed) could be used at weekends for sleepovers so the little one can join in the fun. Likewise, give each child who shares the chance to sleep on his or her own occasionally, in a spare bedroom or on the sofabed. Children, like adults, occasionally need time out from the fray.

THIS PAGE AND OPPOSITE
Offered the chance of bunk beds, most brothers will jump at the chance of sharing, though you can expect inevitable arguments about who gets the top bunk. This room for older boys takes a shared dormitory as its theme. White shutters, no-nonsense floorboards

and utilitarian metal-framed beds all suggest summer camp, while the furniture – a battered sports locker, individual initialled trunks and aluminium chairs – completes the look. If dormitory-style is your chosen theme, shared clothes storage and identical bedding are all part of the fun.

" *I like sharing. But Bc*

kicks my bed! " TUCKER, AGE 11

Plan a practical yet imaginative bathroom, so that the kids' daily ablutions are fun. Aim for a family bathroom that's sophisticated enough for grown-ups but suitable for children, too. Flexible storage and neutral shades are the keys to success.

bath rooms

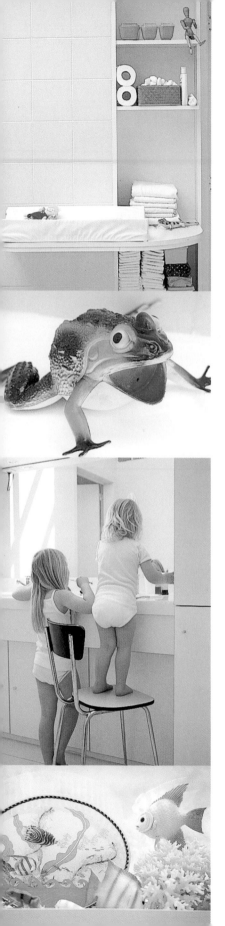

The bathroom is one of the most hard-working spaces in the home. It needs to be efficient enough for the before-school wash and brush-up yet cosy enough to prompt fun-filled bathtimes. In terms of encouraging washing routines, you've won half the battle if the bathroom is a tempting place to spend time.

Most children have a love–hate relationship with their daily ablutions. One week, they will obsessively brush their teeth; the next, they're terrified of the shower. But nearly all little ones find it soothing to take a bath. Around the age of seven, children may choose not to bathe with siblings. Girls prefer splashing around with lotions and potions, while boys would rather be anywhere than in the bathroom.

If possible, give the children their own bathroom, which can double as a guest bathroom. A designated kids' bathroom means you can install splashproof materials, scaled-down sanitaryware and jolly colours, and save more sophisticated details for your own bathroom. But if the room is really tiny, consider other options. Would you be better off creating a family-size bathroom elsewhere, with space for a large bathtub plus comfortable chair? Would the tiny room work better as a toilet and basin, rather than trying to squeeze in a bath as well? Depending on the layout of the house, it might make sense for you to sacrifice your planned en suite bathroom to the family and have a tiny en suite shower room instead. Site the kids' bathroom close to their bedrooms. Slippery, tired children make bathtime chaotic enough, so the nearer they are to their pyjamas the better.

If you are planning to design and build a bathroom from scratch, firstly decide whether to have a bath and separate shower cubicle or a wall-mounted shower attachment over the bathtub. Little ones tend to prefer baths to showers. Some find the pressure of a power-shower uncomfortable on their heads, and they may be frightened by the sheer volume of rushing water.

A shared family bathroom has to please everyone, and with its zingy grapefruit colour scheme and glass skylights, this one does the trick. Always devote as much space as possible to the bathroom, then introduce an invigorating colour scheme and an abundance of light.

Good storage is essential, too. In this bathroom, there are under-sink cupboards as well as out-of-reach units for adults' toiletries. The double basins are ideal for the morning rush. Adding a built-in nappy-changing area is a clever idea, but locate shelving for all the equipment within arm's reach.

THIS PAGE AND OPPOSITE..
Bathtime is much more
enjoyable for children if there
are decorative touches in
the bathroom that appeal to
their imagination. But if a
bathroom is shared with
adults, you can't allow kids'
stuff to take over. The answer
is to keep the decor plain,
using white tiles or tongue-
and-groove panelling, so that
the style appeals to adults
too. Essential details include
a waterproof toy basket and
low shelves for the children's
bubble bath. A wacky shower
curtain is a great way to
inject fun: shimmery silver,
three-dimensional flowers or
pockets for family snaps are
all good. Any extras will be
appreciated, from a funky
bathroom cabinet to a fully
fitted fish tank.

THIS PAGE AND OPPOSITE **In a kids-only bathroom, fitting a small low-level bath and mini-washbasin is an appealing option. Roll-top baths are especially appropriate for children, as there are no sharp edges to bang little heads on.**

Reconditioned Victorian baths are often a good option, as many come in small sizes. Consider siting a bathtub in the middle of the room. It makes getting in and out easier, and there is also less likelihood of the walls getting splashed.

Children love to be independent, and being able to climb in and out of the bath by themselves is a milestone. But if the children's bathroom is to be shared with guests, spare a thought for an adult trying to squeeze into a tiny tub, and think twice before choosing a low, small bath.

Children are more likely to slip if they shower standing up in the bath than in a freestanding cubicle. If an over-bath shower is the only option, buy a non-slip rubber mat and a plastic shower curtain. Probably the best configuration is to site a grown-up power-shower elsewhere in the house, and fit the children's bath with a hand-held shower attachment for washing hair.

Children love to be independent, and being able to climb in and out of the bath by themselves is a milestone. But if the children's bathroom is to be shared with guests, spare a thought for an adult trying to squeeze into a tiny tub and think twice before choosing a low, small bath. A big bathtub has lots of advantages. When siblings bathe together, they appreciate plenty of space for play, while in a family bathroom a generous bath will give you a share of adult luxury. Positioning taps in the centre of a bath means that neither child has to have the tap end.

To cope with the early morning rush, it makes sense to have two (or even three) basins. A row of scaled-down basins is eye-catching, and is a sensible option if space is tight. There are plenty of stylish, practical choices that are ideal for kids. Small stainless-steel bowls set into a stone or wood worktop look ultra-trendy, as do wall-hung white ceramic butler's sinks. A small basin designed for cloakroom use is another option. The appeal of a wall-hung or inset basin is that you can lower the height for kids. For standard-size pedestal sinks, provide a sturdy plastic or wooden stool so children can step up to the correct height.

Little details will give small children the confidence they need to use the bathroom by themselves. Cross-head or lever taps are easier to handle than round knobs, while a mixer tap will guard against scalds from the hot tap. Wall-mounted taps are easier to keep clean than basin-fitted ones. A counter with an inset basin provides space for washroom essentials. If the basin is freestanding, fit a tooth mug in a wall-mounted holder, so it can't be knocked over, and replace soap bars with liquid soap in a dispenser. Think about the toilet. A wall-hung model can be sited lower down. Is the handle too stiff for little fingers? Would a push-button mechanism be better? If you have room, install a large heated towel rail. There's nothing worse than being enfolded in yesterday's damp towel.

Make your bathroom one hundred per cent splashproof now, and you won't mind about water fights later. Appealing floor options include non-slip rubber tiles in bright colours as well as linoleum and vinyl. Cork floor tiles with PVC laminate finish also come in water-themed designs such as sand and shells. Sealed or painted wooden boards are also suitable, though wood laminates are sensitive to deluges of bath water. Stone, such as limestone or slate, is smart, waterproof and, if you install underfloor heating, feels fabulous underfoot. However, it does get slippery when wet, so invest in a cosy absorbent bathmat. Children will also adore a concrete floor studded with pebbles and little shells, which also has plenty of grip.

The walls will get splashed with lots of water so floor-to-ceiling tiles are sensible. In a kids-only bathroom, big, square tiles in a cheerful shade look graphic and modern. For a co-ordinated look,

BELOW LEFT Small details, such as a colourful toilet seat, can transform a small, all-white bathroom.

BELOW RIGHT Surfaces must be robust and easy to clean. Vividly coloured laminates make attractive panels and surrounds, while stone, from slate to marble, is practical as well as stylish.

THIS PAGE **The ultimate luxury in a kids-only bathroom is that sinks can be situated at child height. Don't forget to include a stool for adults to perch on while supervising bathtime.**

THIS PAGE **In a bathroom shared by adults and kids, a cast-iron bath adds a touch of luxury. When installing a shower, choose an outsize shower tray or build a 'wet' shower, so all the kids can squeeze in together. If you are fitting a power-shower, choose a shower head with the option for a gentler spray.**

OPPOSITE **Provide steps or a sturdy stool so little ones, such as five-year-old Gussie, can reach a high basin comfortably.**

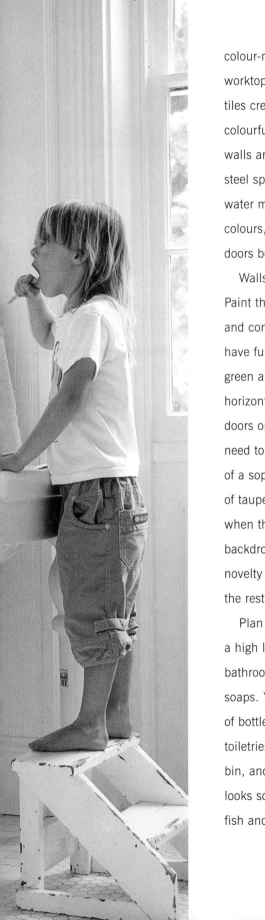

colour-match them with a painted wooden floor or laminate worktops. In a shared family bathroom, subway-style white brick tiles create a more sophisticated look, but work just as well with colourful bath toys as with adult accessories. Limestone-clad walls are another grown-up option, but resist glass and stainless-steel splashbacks. They may look chic, but will show every water mark. Laminates, which are available in a host of enticing colours, are another good choice for bath panels and cupboard doors beneath vanity units.

Walls can also be lined with tongue-and-groove or MDF panels. Paint them and the walls in eggshell, which resists splash marks and condensation well. If your sanitaryware is white, you can have fun with colour on the walls. Jazzy shades such as grass green and turquoise are particularly appropriate. Paint broad horizontal stripes on walls or use colour to delineate different doors on built-in cupboards. In a shared family bathroom, you need to design a chameleon-like colour scheme. The combination of a sophisticated surface like limestone with a restful palette of taupe, lilac or eau-de-Nil guarantees a bathroom that's adult when the children's things are put away, yet is still an appropriate backdrop for plastic bath toys. Steer kids away from garish novelty character towels, and provide plain ones that complement the rest of the room.

Plan plenty of storage for bathroom paraphernalia, including a high lockable cabinet for any medicines. In a shared family bathroom, give the kids a cupboard for novelty bubble baths and soaps. You won't have to share your grown-up soak with a jumble of bottles, and surfaces are easier to keep clean when free of toiletries. The same principle applies to toys: provide a big plastic bin, and after bathtime they can be tidied away so the space looks sophisticated again. In a kids-only bathroom, display plastic fish and submarines on shelves above the bath.

play spaces

Play – be it energetic or peaceful – is the centralizing force in a child's life, so kids need space to scoot around and spread their toys about. Adults need to be able to tidy it all away. Storage that works is the key.

6

THIS PAGE AND OPPOSITE
With a bit of forethought, a wonderful play space can be seamlessly integrated into an open-plan living area. Modern flooring materials such as limestone are perfect surfaces for toys, and, with the addition of underfloor heating, are warm and comfortable to play on. If you are planning a play space from scratch, doors to an outside space are a worthwhile investment. Storage should be streamlined and unobtrusive. In Pablo's play space, shown here, capacious sliding drawers allow him easy access to his toys.

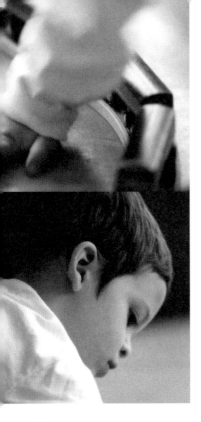

Every child needs space to play. An expanse of floor, a freshly cleared tabletop and enough room to race around are the essentials – without these, children have no free rein with their toys. As adults, we allocate ourselves activity zones: a sofa to sprawl on, a desk for paying bills, an armchair for reading. Children need their own equivalent. It's not fair to tell children they can play all over the house, only to scold them for piling toys on the stairs. Try to give your kids a special area where they know they can play. Size isn't the issue. Whether it's a patch of floor within a kitchen/dining room or a separate playroom, what's important is that this is a space they can call their own. Make toys accessible and easy to tidy away, and kids will even enjoy organizing their own private zone.

In recent years, many families have devoted their largest living space to a kitchen, dining and playroom all rolled into one. In a conventional house or flat, an open-plan area is easily created by knocking down walls. But industrial loft conversions are increasingly on the agenda. A decade ago, lofts were the province of the trendy and the child-free. But those same couples are now having families and enjoying the benefits of a vast area of one-level floor space. A loft or warehouse space creates the ultimate indoor playground, with ample room for bike-riding and space-hopping.

The advantages of an open-plan living space are manifold. Toddlers can safely play under a grown-up's watchful eye while cooking, watching videos and older kids' homework all get under way. If you're moving house to accommodate a growing family, this is the ideal space configuration to aim for. It's helpful to have a toilet nearby, so little ones don't have to travel far. And, if possible, access from the living area/play space to a garden or roof terrace is invaluable. In summer, it doubles the available floor area, while in winter the kids might be more easily tempted outdoors.

> 66 *This is a really big space for my trains. I like playing here because I'm next to mummy when she's in the kitchen.* 99
>
> PABLO, AGE 3½

If you can't move house but are adapting your living quarters to accommodate children, think long and hard about the changes you make. You will reap the benefits of employing an architect, although it may seem a major investment at the time. An architect will think laterally about maximizing space and can squeeze storage into the most unlikely corners. Alternatively, if finances are tight, can rooms be swapped around? Perhaps a dining room off the kitchen could be converted into a playroom, or an under-used conservatory adapted into a kids' den?

However, if you have a spare room away from the living area that might be converted into a separate playroom, think twice about doing so when your children are small. You won't want to be cooking while having to keep half an ear open for what's going on next door, and life is infinitely easier if you don't have to call a halt to exciting play in one room and move children to the kitchen to eat. Far better to include the kids' play area within the bosom of the house and get on with the riotous business of family life.

The area chosen for a play space needs to provide a decent amount of floor area for spreading out toys as well as enough room to run around. Make sure anything else going on in the same space won't interfere with the kids' activities, and vice versa. Could you re-route traffic through a play area by moving a sofa to one side of the room? Will you be forever tripping over toddlers while trying to prepare food?

If the play space is within or adjacent to the kitchen, safety is vital. Clip trailing wires and cushion sharp corners. Install cupboards with child locks and plugs with safety covers, and always, always tuck in saucepan handles.

The disadvantage of sharing a living space with children is that they bring a sea of brightly coloured plastic with them. It's natural to worry that their arrival may threaten the integrity of your home,

" *It was a way to prevent toys cluttering up the floor.* "

FRIEDA, MOTHER

THIS PAGE AND OPPOSITE
While lofts and kids generally go together well, it helps adults and children to be tidy if one area is designated as the toy zone. Where there is a very large floor area, building a child-height maze from painted MDF partitions makes good sense, as Juliet and Lucie's parents found out. Make it big enough to hold several little 'rooms' where toy shops or dolls' houses can be permanently located. Painted a strong colour and set amid white walls, the maze will become a talking point for adults and a magnet for kids.

yet a minimal interior needn't disappear for ever. Rule number one is to provide effective storage so that in the evenings toys can be put away quickly and easily, and order restored for the benefit of the adults. The best solution is to kit out your living/play space with floor-to-ceiling cupboards with flush doors and deep shelves. Locate the kids' things on the lower shelves and use the upper ones for household paraphernalia. If you can, specify extra-deep cupboards so that fold-up dolls' buggies or plastic garages can fit in easily. If there's no room for cupboards, and open shelves are the only option, invest in some decent-looking containers that look good en masse. Clear plastic crates and wicker baskets are both practical and stylish.

Rule number two is that precious or beautiful pieces should be put into storage or placed firmly out of reach. If you have the luxury of a adults-only sitting room, enjoy your prized possessions in there. It's easy to teach children to respect lovely things and not to draw on the walls, but sensible to accept that accidents will happen. So protect your cherrywood dining table with a wipe-clean PVC cloth and your expensively upholstered sofa with a loose cover in a tough, washable fabric. Replace a limited-edition rug with an abstract one from a chain store. Beaded cushions, velvet throws or anything else labelled 'dry-clean only' should be removed. Remember, you're creating a child-friendly zone so that everyone can relax.

If you've moved house, decorating and furnishing a play space that doubles as a family living room is great fun. The beauty of integrating kids' stuff with contemporary design is that trendy industrial-style surfaces like stainless steel, plywood and laminate are smart and hard-wearing, and the clear, bright colours of much modern furniture are positively enhanced when littered with toys. When decorating walls, white vinyl matt emulsion creates a simple background, and scuff marks are easily touched up.

OPPOSITE, ABOVE **Every play space needs comfortable seating for chilling out in front of the television or reading. A simple banquette, like this one, can incorporate drawers for small toys and jigsaws.**

OPPOSITE, BELOW **As an alternative to the ubiquitous miniature table and chairs, a wood or MDF desktop, fixed on an adjustable rack, provides a corner for quiet play or drawing and writing, and can be made higher as the child grows.**

LEFT **In a large living room, try to incorporate desk space for older children, for homework, doing practical projects or using a laptop computer.**

PREVIOUS PAGES **With a little judicious selection, there are plenty of playful features that remain easy on the eye once installed in a sophisticated adult space. The key is to use them with confidence, scale them up, and choose colours that will positively enhance the grown-up scheme. Thus, a blackboard can take up half the wall (useful for shopping lists or phone messages), and beanbags can be adult-size and chic with it, perhaps in leather or vinyl. Appropriately placed, a toy such as a bright red child's swing suspended from the ceiling can have as much decorative impact as a contemporary chair.**

THIS PAGE AND OPPOSITE **If space and your budget allow, a child-size heated indoor swimming pool provides kids with the ultimate play space and, if fitted with a swimming current for adults, can be used by the whole family. The parents of these children have positioned a big, comfortable sofa beyond the splashproof glass doors, so an adult can supervise in comfort.**

You can have plenty of fun with colour too. A single wall painted in vibrant lime green or dazzling bright blue can look stunning, particularly if decorated with children's artwork that has been properly framed and displayed.

Practical furniture makes life much easier. Polypropylene chairs are a sensible, easy-clean option and 1960s-style versions in vivid tangerine and lime green are wonderfully appealing. If a table doubles as a dining and painting table, a wipe-clean surface is essential, so a laminated top is ideal. If the table needs to be pushed to one side to create more space, add castors and the look becomes more fashionable still. To house items of electronic equipment, choose a long cabinet instead of open shelves. If you have a steel one powder-coated in shocking pink, you will be making a design statement at the same time.

You can be similarly imaginative when selecting fabric for the playroom sofa or chairs. Several bright plains can look stunningly abstract if used as blocks of colour on individual chairs, seats and cushions. Leather is durable and stylish as well as ultra-practical because it is wipe-clean.

Patterned fabric is excellent for disguising sticky finger marks. Source something bold and wacky that will appeal to both you and the kids: giant cabbage roses on a slim steel-legged sofa, or a 1950s pictorial print of seaside scenes. When it comes to decorating a play space, you can be a little tongue-in-cheek. A 1970s swivel chair upholstered in Mr Men fabric would look funky, as might a giant abstract painting which blurs the barriers between modern art and kids' naïve efforts.

Every play space needs a cosy corner for watching a DVD or listening to music. If space permits, a small sofa is great for naps or quiet reading; if there's no room, beanbags work equally well. Play spaces in communal living areas often have hard wood or limestone floors, so a rug or a fluffy faux animal-print throw provides a softer sitting or crawling area for babies and toddlers.

Keep the television out of the way by mounting it on a wall bracket or a pull-out arm concealed within a cupboard. But try to site the video or DVD player at child level, since even very young children will relish the independence of being able to insert their favourite film. Provide plenty of storage for CDs and DVDs nearby. They can be stacked in plastic crates or a narrow section of custom-made shelving.

If you're blessed with abundant living space, you can include a few wacky extras. Consider hanging a swing from the ceiling or keeping a pop-up tent or play house permanently erected.

OPPOSITE, ABOVE LEFT AND RIGHT AND BELOW RIGHT
Kids glory in the luxury of plenty of play space, yet the adults in these three homes haven't been forced to make decorative compromises. The modern classic furniture, sofas in bright colours and casual floor cushions are as trendy as they are child-friendly, so everyone benefits.

OPPOSITE, BELOW LEFT
A sophisticated adult sitting room can be made family-orientated by incorporating washable covers and stain-guarded upholstery. Molly and Eli have soon learned what they can and can't touch.

OPPOSITE, BELOW CENTRE
When a living room doubles as a play space, there must be plenty of storage. Nica keeps toys in the retro sideboard and 1970s stacking compartments.

OPPOSITE **With their vast
expanses of floor space, city
lofts are wonderful for children.
There's even room to ride a bike,
so, on rainy days, kids can burn
off energy at home. Johanna's
parents have a side sitting area
where they can relax while
watching the children.**

THIS PAGE **A long, comfortable
sofa, big enough to seat the
whole family, makes an ideal
centrepiece, but for practicality
choose strongly coloured
upholstery or a busy pattern
to conceal spills and stains.**

spaces to eat

Little ones need a calm and comfortable spot where they can eat beneath your watchful gaze. Choose wipe-clean furniture and scaled-down shapes, with plates and cutlery in jelly-bean shades, and you'll tempt even the most reluctant eater to the table.

7

It's common for children to gather in the kitchen, so if you're planning a new kitchen make it a stimulating place to be. This example was deliberately designed with small children in mind. Ease of use is paramount. The long bar handles are simple for kids to grab, and their plates and cups are located in a low cupboard. Island units make sense: children can gather round and help to cook, eat meals there, or sit and draw pictures. Include plenty of drawers, so that napkins, straws and place mats are easy for kids to reach.

Children's mealtimes may seem like feeding time at the zoo, but, if you choose practical yet good-looking furniture and equipment, cleaning up should be relatively quick. In the early years, babies progress rapidly from being spoon-fed to helping themselves in a highchair, then graduating to the adults' table. Whatever stage they're at, the process of getting kids to sit down, eat calmly and observe table manners needs to be achieved with minimum fuss and maximum efficiency. If there is a comfortable eating area, and food is presented appealingly, recalcitrant eaters are more likely to hop up to the table.

If possible, situate the table in the kitchen, so you can keep an eye on the kids while preparing food or clearing up. The advantages are obvious. You are on the spot if a child chokes; the kitchen floor is practical and wipe-clean; and food, drink and a damp cloth for sticky faces are all close to hand.

Don't despair at the thought that your high-tech modern kitchen will be spoiled by highchairs and bright crockery. If you source attractive furniture and kitchenware, the transition will be seamless. Colourful seating, a lime-green toaster and pink plastic beakers will only pep up a stainless-steel kitchen.

It's fun to provide little ones with a diminutive table and chairs at which they can eat meals or draw and paint. Good-looking styles include miniature versions of the classic Arne Jacobsen 'Ant' chair.

A highchair is essential for babies. Standard designs are practical, but often rather an eyesore. You can either accept this and put up with it or source a more attractive option. There are simple wooden Scandinavian designs available, or plain white lacquered-steel versions. Alternatively, look for a second-hand highchair. Repaint it in a bold colour and re-cover the seat in a retro-print oilcloth. You may need to add new safety straps.

If you have older kids who eat at the main table, a sturdy canvas or plastic clip-on seat is sociable for older babies, because it attaches directly onto the tabletop and enables them to interact. You might also consider a highchair designed to grow up with the child. These often come in smart chrome and beech. They feature a clip-on tray and safety guard for the baby stage, then adapt into a seat for older children, leaving just a useful footrest.

THIS PAGE AND OPPOSITE
It's nice to give children the option of eating at the dining table or at their own special miniature table. Choose a big family table, so there's always room for friends, and select a tough tabletop to withstand spills and scratches. Good materials include zinc, stainless steel, cement, marble, slate and laminate. Save the designer chairs for later years. For a growing family, it's more fun to have mismatched wooden chairs, painted in fun colours, or comfortably upholstered ones with washable covers.

THIS PAGE AND OPPOSITE
It makes sense to think of the children's plates and cutlery as an extension of the adults' options, so the table looks co-ordinated. Scour the shops for trendy, informal tableware that everyone can share: jewel-coloured tumblers, hand-painted bowls (this page) and ceramic mugs (opposite, below right), ideal for both milk or a cup of coffee. Here, Harry enjoys his cereal from an adult pudding bowl (opposite, below centre). Children love pottery-painting cafés, where they have the opportunity to customize their own cups and plates. And buying a picnic set with jolly-coloured plates and bowls has a dual function: the kids can use it both on a day-to-day basis and for family outings.

It's fun to provide little ones with a diminutive table and chairs at which they can eat meals or draw and paint. However, if you like to sit with the kids while they eat, you may not find it such a comfortable option. Eating at a breakfast bar or adding a low countertop to the end of an island unit might be a more practical solution. The choice of small-scale tables and chairs has increased recently; look in high-street stores, children's equipment catalogues or adult contemporary design emporia. Good-looking styles include miniature versions of the classic Arne Jacobsen 'Ant' chair, chunky wooden seats in primary colours and whitewashed Swedish-style tables and benches. You can match the style to your kitchen.

The sooner you encourage small children to sit up at the grown-ups' table the better; it socializes them and fosters a sense of independence. If you have a beautiful table, protect it with a PVC tablecloth. The same goes for upholstered dining chairs. It may sound like an expensive option to have a set of loose covers made up, but it means that the upholstery will be saved from sticky fingers. When choosing new chairs for family mealtimes, look for polypropylene, metal or wood. Light chairs in plastic or

ABOVE LEFT AND RIGHT
Retro highchairs are by far the most tasteful versions on offer, so scour junk shops for old wooden models that can be enlivened with gloss paint or fitted with a new tray. Choose a style that harmonizes with the other chairs around the table.

aluminium are good, because a small child can manoeuvre one around by himself. Pick a style that is comfortable for children as well as looking chic. A slatted seat can trap fingers, while a chair with arms won't pull close enough to the table for a small person to eat in comfort. School-style benches are also excellent, providing plenty of extra room for friends. High stools at a breakfast bar are wonderful for older children, but take care to ensure that little ones don't overbalance.

With imaginative shopping, you and the children will find laying the table a positively creative experience. Tiny versions of anything will delight the kids, and a choice of colours is great, because each can pick their favourite shade. Not everything has to be plastic, although picnic sets in Dayglo colours are a good source of plates and cups. Duralex glass tumblers are virtually indestructible and come in appealingly small sizes. Many casual

dining ranges are in robust pottery, and traditional enamel plates and cups are also hard-wearing. These days, many manufacturers produce bright-handled cutlery in small sizes.

Customize place mats by drawing on slate slabs with chalks or transferring a favourite photograph onto mats at a specialist store. Alternatively, scour design shops for wacky wipe-clean place mats and pictorial napkins.

Everything to do with kids' mealtimes should be accessible for them, as it encourages setting the table from an early age. Store bowls and cutlery in a low cupboard and drawer. Is the fridge easy for an older child to open, so they can help themselves to snacks? Is there a sturdy stool for a little one to hop onto so he can get a drink of water from the tap? The easier you make eating and drinking for your children, the sooner they will be integrated into the sociable world of family mealtimes.

ABOVE LEFT AND RIGHT
Miniature table-and-chair sets needn't be clumsy pieces of moulded plastic in garish colours. For an individual and stylish look, choose more elegant versions that mimic modern classics, such as these moulded beech-veneer 1960s-style chairs (above left).

Call it paraphernalia, equipment, toys or simply stuff, children have an alarming number of possessions, which can all too easily clutter up a home. If the whole family is to co-exist in peace and harmony, it's up to you to squeeze efficient storage out of every tiny space.

spaces for storage

8

THIS PAGE **When a bedroom is also a playroom, cupboard doors that conceal toys will guarantee more restful bedtimes. In this loft, Plexiglass and plywood cupboards are used throughout, not just in the child's room.**

OPPOSITE **Capacious drawers hold toys and are easy to reach. Be imaginative with the drawer fronts: cut out patterns from MDF fronts or choose stainless-steel or painted wood fascias.**

New parents soon learn that children are constantly accompanied by lots of stuff. Over the years, regular clear-outs will help, but the fact remains that the minute you start a family your need for hard-working storage increases tenfold. After the baby bouncer and sit-on fire engine come fleets of tiny cars and dolls' accessories, then home-made models, musical instruments, tennis rackets and more. Accept the influx with good grace, and set about planning where everything should go. It's a cliché, but a place for everything is the ultimate aim, even if frenetic family life doesn't allow for an 'everything in its place' conclusion.

However capacious the storage in the children's bedrooms and play space, there will be yet more stuff you need to house in heavy-traffic areas like the entrance hall. Ask yourself where outdoor gear – coats, hats, kiddie umbrellas, boots and buggies – will go. What about sports equipment – ballet and swimming bags, footballs and cricket bats? The older children get, the bigger the kit becomes. Bikes need a home, as do tents, sleeping bags and outdoor games.

If there is room in your hall, a run of cupboards will hold all the essentials and keep things tidy. Consider wall-mounting them, leaving room beneath for shoe storage. For small children, a low row of pegs on the wall is better: outdoor gear can be seen at a glance and little ones may be more inclined to hang up their bags. Use a big basket or galvanized-metal tub to hold shoes, and another for hats, scarves and gloves. A low bench where children can perch while doing up their shoes should be situated near the coat rack. Pick one with a lift-up lid and extra storage within. If bikes are a problem and the hall is high enough, fit them onto a wall rack. Alternatively, store them in the garden or build a lock-up store at the front of the house.

In the long, narrow halls typical of nineteenth-century houses, there's space for little more than peg rails and an umbrella stand.

PREVIOUS PAGES **Large cupboards and deep shelves are essential for storing toys, but just as crucial are plenty of individual containers. They allow kids to organize their toys, so there are homes for pens, plastic animals, building blocks, books, toy cars and so on. Anything can be pressed into service as a container, from galvanized-metal buckets to sisal baskets. See-at-a-glance storage is the most helpful, so choose wicker baskets, transparent plastic crates or screw-topped glass jars. Label everything, so both adults and kids know what lives where.**

ABOVE RIGHT **If you're planning a family home from scratch, a separate corridor running along the side of the house can be devoted to bikes, outdoor gear and sports equipment. Here, wall-mounted cupboards create a sense of order.**

OPPOSITE **Even in a small hall, provide a child-sized stool or bench so children can sit down and take their boots and shoes on and off.**

So storage must be squeezed in elsewhere – perhaps in an understairs cupboard – or take the form of shelves and cupboards in the play area. Don't expect everyday gear to be stored in the children's bedrooms: you need everything to hand for the early-morning rush. However, an array of hanging bags and coats will look messy in an open-plan living and play area. A smart solution is to build a grid system of shelves, each just big enough to hold a labelled wicker basket, and pack everything in. Perhaps a cupboard in the utility room could hold outdoor gear, while open shelves by the back door are good for shoe storage.

In the kitchen/living/play space, it's essential that you and the children have enough storage for day-to-day paraphernalia so that everyone stays organized. Display the school calendar, reading lists and sports fixtures on a giant pinboard, and if its messy appearance spoils a chic dining area, hang it on the inside of a cupboard door. If the play zone is part of the kitchen, clear a kitchen cupboard or drawer so that hairgrips and brushes, museum pamphlets, painting equipment and Play-Doh are easily tidied away yet can be found when needed. If you are planning a

THIS PAGE AND OPPOSITE **Tailor-made storage may seem like an indulgence, but it makes daily activities such as nappy changing and getting the children dressed much simpler. Lots of little compartments are the key to good organization. List the things to be stored, from cotton-wool balls to baby vests, then provide equally well-regimented cubbyholes. Stack see-at-a-glance glass-fronted cabinets with open-topped storage boxes, line a shelf with wicker baskets, or make a decorative feature out of labelling individual drawers. Customize wherever possible: if a cupboard lacks enough compartments, then add your own MDF divisions.**

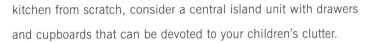

kitchen from scratch, consider a central island unit with drawers and cupboards that can be devoted to your children's clutter.

Built-in storage needs to look fabulous as well as being practical – so design it as an integral part of your decorating scheme, not as an afterthought. If you have one baby now, double the storage you've planned because it will all be used eventually. For the smartest, neatest look, fit doors on all your shelves. They can be wide and sliding or narrow and flush, with finishes in everything from painted MDF to sand-blasted glass, zinc, Perspex or wood. Avoid open shelves. Lovely as they look when just built, the clean, clutter-free look will be gone once they are crammed with toys, books and equipment. Use every spare inch of space. Floor-level drawers are great for toys, while a narrow alcove can hold bookshelves. There's still a place for freestanding furniture, but go for quirky pieces that add character, like an old metal sports locker.

There's no point having good storage if children won't use it. Make it so simple for them that there can be no arguments. Handles should be easy to grip, so look for metal D-handles, recessed door-pulls and chunky knobs. Keep some shelves shallow, so that items don't get lost at the back. Within a cupboard, divide up paper, pens, scissors and glues within small plastic crates, sisal baskets or good old-fashioned baked-bean cans. Compartmentalize drawers with shop-bought dividers or make your own from sections of MDF. And label boxes and crates. If the children can't read yet, use a Polaroid picture of each toy type for reference, or colour-coding: red for books, blue for cars, and so on.

When an activity comes to an end, teach your children to put everything away before they start the next game. It's a lesson that we adults could do well to learn, too!

Kids love outdoor spaces, where they can run, jump and play crazy games. Give them a secret hideaway and they'll disappear for hours. It doesn't matter whether you have a modest city garden or huge lawns – any outdoor space allows children to let off steam.

outdoor spaces

9

Let children loose in an open space and they're off, tearing about with all the delight of a puppy off the leash. If properly wrapped up, they rarely notice if it's cold and the grass is wet, and on a summer's day will happily stay outdoors till dusk. Try to give them some outside space. We can't all have vast lawns, but even a tiny backyard or roof terrace has potential for creative play.

The current obsession among designers with developing the indoor–outdoor principle offers many benefits for children, and can provide the perfect solution in a small urban patch. An indoor play space that opens straight onto the garden makes outdoors very accessible. Children can run in and out and are easily visible to adults within.

If your property is not suitable for this arrangement, consider the exit points from the house. Ideally, kids should be able to get in and out by themselves, so French windows or sliding doors are ideal. If the only access to the outside is through a 'precious' adult sitting room with a carpeted floor, could you create a new door, perhaps via a utility room or the kitchen?

The whole point about children playing outside is that they should be able to do so unaccompanied – it's no fun playing

cowboys and Indians with a grown-up standing by. Tiny ones do need a more watchful eye, however. Before you let them loose, make sure children will be absolutely safe. Fit the back gate with a lock and check they can't climb over the fence or fall over the edge of a roof terrace. Are all swings, ropes and treehouse ladders secure and well-supported? Water features, from a tiny pond to a swimming pool, must be made child-safe too.

Somehow, you need to make the children feel that they are free while still keeping a close watch on what they're up to. One option is to create a screen separating a children's play area at the bottom of the garden from the rest of the lawn. Construct it from large-scale trellis or bamboo, so that you can see through the gaps. And a treehouse should be visible from at least one window in the house.

A playhouse is always a winner. Children love the idea of a private space of their own, and they can store all their outside toys there. There's no need to spoil your garden with a garish plastic structure: the wooden variety is much more tasteful. However, custom-made children's cottages can be ruinously expensive. It is far better to design your own and get a carpenter to make it, or even to adapt an ordinary garden shed. As long as the structure has a door and windows, it will be heaven for little girls and boys. Reach a stylistic compromise on the decoration. If you choose to paint the exterior in a subtle colour like lichen green, allow the kids to design the inside. Use a staple gun to staple fabric remnants to the inside of windows for curtains, and add little chairs and tables.

If your budget permits, a more sophisticated summer house can be fitted with water, electricity and heating. It could even double up as a home office or guest room.

A treehouse or a simple raised platform between branches will double the appeal of being outdoors. You could make it to

THIS PAGE AND OPPOSITE
Nothing beats the appeal of an outdoor playhouse. It's relatively simple to adapt a shop-bought DIY wooden shed, customizing it with a gingerbread roof trim or a stable-style door. Ensure the playhouse is waterproof, then help your children decorate the inside, perhaps with a painted wooden floor or even wallpaper. For proper imaginative play, the house must have a window and a door. Fit in chairs and a table, and supply galvanized-metal bins or wicker baskets for chucking toys into at the end of the day.

scaled-down proportions, so that only kids can squeeze through the opening into their 'house'. Or build it big enough for the whole family to enjoy an evening meal up there. Apart from ladders, all sorts of extras can be added. Suspend a hammock, hang a string of Chinese lanterns, a rope ladder, climbing rope or a swing. While a treehouse blends best into the tree if built from hardwood, you could paint it a bright colour and turn it into the central focus of the garden.

When planning child-friendly outdoor space, divide up the available space into specific activity areas, using a scale plan if necessary. Ideally, there should be a running-about area, a deck designated for a table and chairs, and a secret play area, perhaps with a sandpit, usually at the end of the garden. If you have older boys, you might instead want to allocate the bottom of the garden for football. Keep their scuffed piece of lawn out of sight by disguising it with a dividing section of wall or fence. In a

THIS PAGE AND OPPOSITE
By adding imaginative features to
your garden, you will fire your
children's imagination. A densely
planted area, with a mirror on
one wall, becomes a fairy grotto
at the bottom of the garden,
while a trompe-l'oeil gate
suggests a secret world beyond.
Break up a boring expanse of
lawn with pretty picket fencing or
fast-growing plants like bamboo,
so there are secret spots for a
private picnic or games of hide-
and-seek. Always secure any
exits from the garden so everyone
is safe. Provide children with
fun equipment so that playing
outdoors becomes an extension of
inside. Here, Yasmin and Sarah
let off steam with a giant ball.

bold contemporary garden, the wall could be turned into an
architectural feature and painted in a vibrant hue. Alternatively,
integrate it into the rest of the garden by growing a flowering
creeper over it, and fit with a pretty wall-mounted fountain. Think
about imaginative ways to mark out the different activity areas.
You could use tall plants, set stepping stones into the lawn or put
up a trellis. And, although a vast manicured lawn is great for
running around on, and an ideal spot for the trampoline or
climbing frame, kids do appreciate a touch of nature's chaos.
Section off a part of the garden, plant it with bamboo, palms,
wild grasses and flowers, and you won't see your kids for dust.

Such divisions are impossible in a very small outdoor area,
so concentrate instead on making the space attractive for adults
yet user-friendly for kids. Laying the same flooring throughout
instantly unifies a tiny garden: limestone, wood decking, quarry
tiles and cement are all good options. Don't sacrifice running-
about space by having large flowerbeds: stick to robust, evergreen

> " *Friends come over and the children can do their thing – having a pool is the greatest form of entertainment.* "

shrubs in tubs, which not only look stylish but will also withstand the odd knock from a football. Hard surfaces are practical, but children also appreciate a spot of grass where they can flop down and read. A circle of turf, however small, can look very chic surrounded by limestone flagstones, and allows sufficient space to pitch a tiny tent.

Provide access to sand and water in the garden, and you'll keep younger children amused for hours. Shop-bought sandpits frequently come in garish colours, so consider building your own. If you are creating a small city garden from scratch, a sandpit can be inset into the hard floor, but fit a tight cover over it so that sand is protected at night. An outdoor tap/faucet that is easy enough for a child to turn on means that little ones can fill buckets or water the garden to their hearts' content. It's relatively easy to plumb in a hot-water tap too. if you add a giant planter beneath it, the children can indulge in a marvellous hot bath in the open air. With safety in mind, it is advisable not to have a fish pond until your children reach their teenage years. But it's still possible to enjoy water features: choose a wall-mounted fountain

PREVIOUS PAGES **A great child-friendly garden has a structure to climb on, a quiet area and a stretch of grass to run around on. Relaxed planting means kids don't have to steer clear of special flowers – or you can teach them to respect the garden by giving them their own patch. If there's no natural shade, provide a sun umbrella or little tent, or grow a creeper over an arch.**

THIS PAGE AND OPPOSITE **Well-supervised kids can spend hours playing in water. Provide inflatable boats and animals, plus flippers and snorkels, and blow-up rings for younger ones. For Bo, Tucker, Gibson and Gussie, the pool is the place to be.**

THIS PAGE AND OPPOSITE
Instead of fretting about the limitations of a small, urban outdoor space, concentrate instead on finding enjoyable ways to equip it for play. With a water pipe, paddling pool and hose, this small rooftop eyrie is an irresistible draw for three-year-old Teresa on a hot day. Water-play equipment is cheap and fun: look out for giant water pistols, or spray and jet attachments for a conventional garden sprinkler. Pick a rigid rather than blow-up style of paddling pool, as it will double as a sandpit.

with a self-circulating pump, so that the water goes round and
round, instead of pooling into a potentially fatal trough.

Eating outdoors is exciting for children and fun for adults too.
Choose all-weather metal or wooden furniture that can be left out
all year round, so that impromptu alfresco meals are easy. Look
for miniature versions of teak garden furniture or tiny deckchairs
in bright canvas. Building a wooden arbour for trailing flowering
plants or a vine provides essential shade. And a family barbecue,
beneath its leafy cover, is the stuff childhood memories are made of.

stockists and suppliers

UK

ONE-STOP SHOPS

Ikea
www.ikea.com
Fresh, affordable designs for the nursery and children's bedrooms including beds, junior chairs and tables, novelty lighting and textiles.

Laura Ashley
www.lauraashley.com
Co-ordinating fabrics, wallpaper and bed sets in soft colours, for babies, boys and girls, plus accessories in traditional styles from rugs to storage boxes.

Mothercare
www.mothercare.com
Classic and modern furniture in white or timber, including cots and cot beds, a wide range of bed linen sets, changing units and storage.

Next
www.classic.next.co.uk
Nursery, boy and girl furniture sets, as well as fun bed linen ranges and everyday essentials such as towels and mattresses.

ONLINE STORES

Great Little Trading Company
www.gltc.co.uk
0844 848 6000
Mail-order suppliers of colourful bookcases, storage and children's room accessories.

Kids Rooms
www.kidsrooms.co.uk
Basic, jolly furniture from nursery to teens, including animal chairs and scaled-down sofas for playrooms.

Nubie
www.nubie.co.uk
+ 44 (0)1825 724160
Online modern kids boutique with stock from around the world. Furniture includes cool changing tables, cots and nursing chairs, open plan shelving and contemporary high chairs.

WALLS

Brume
www.brume.co.uk
+ 44 (0)1364 73951
Decorative wall stickers for kids, with seaside, skateboard, animal and typographical motifs, plus made-to-measure window film.

Hibou Home
www.hibouhome.com
+ 44 (0)1580 243188
Designer kids' wallpapers in soft colours including cactus and gymkhana designs.

Isak
www.isak.co.uk
Crisp kids wallpapers with Swedish-influenced motifs including penguins, houses and alphabet letters. Family-friendly accessories include trays, textiles and porcelain sets.

Mini Moderns
www.minimoderns.com
Wallpapers and matching fabrics with a retro vibe in mid-century colours, designed to appeal to adults and kids alike. Motifs include boats, birdcages, chairs and musical instruments, with matching cushions.

Olive Loves Alfie
www.olivelovesalfie.co.uk
+ 44 (0)20 7241 4212
100% VOC-free paints in bright and pastel shades and matt and gloss finishes, designed for the family home.

Paperboy
www.paperboywallpaper.co.uk
+ 44 (0)20 7193 9135
Wallpaper and fabrics specifically for boys. Fun colours and jolly designs including spaceships, jigsaw pieces, dragons and spitfires.

FABRICS

Designers Guild
www.designersguild.com
+ 44 (0)20 7893 7400
Fabrics in vibrant colours and whimsical motifs, plus co-ordinating bedding, cushions, rugs and wallpapers.

Emily Bond
www.emilybond.co.uk
+ 44 (0)1173 763067
English cottons and linens with cute farmyard and dog motifs, and a children's collection featuring seagulls, planes and stars.

Ian Mankin
www.ianmankin.co.uk
+ 44 (0)20 7722 0997
A brilliant source of striped and plain cottons, linens, indigo denims and oilcloths, plus beanbags and lighting.

FURNITURE

Aspace
www.aspace.co.uk,
A huge selection of single, high sleeper and sofa beds for kids in a choice of paint finishes and timbers. Colourful storage options and desks for all ages.

Bump
www.bumpstuff.com
+ 44 (0)20 7249 7000
Classic range of children's beds in single/nursery, day, trundle and double sizes, in a choice of styles from sleigh to country beds. They arrive flat-packed and unpainted; mattresses available.

The Conran Shop
www.conranshop.co.uk,
The iconic design shop stocks colourful furniture for kids including scaled down versions of classic 20th-century designs, beanbags and mini bentwood chairs in bright colours.

The Dormy House
www.thedormyhouse.com
+ 44 (0)1264 365808
An inventive selection of classic beds with sleepover under beds, multi-modular and under-bed storage crates, noticeboards and desks.

Feather & Black
www.featherandblack.com
+ 44 (0)1243 380 600
A great range of painted and timber children's beds, bunk beds and bed/storage systems, and matching chests of drawers and desks. Also colourful lamps and beanbags.

Molly Meg
www.molly-meg.co.uk
+ 44 (0)7971 691327
Online design shop for children with fantastic selection of modern and vintage scaled down furniture, plus wall decoration, groovy toys and cushions.

BED LINEN
Caramel Baby and Child
www.caramel-shop.co.uk
291 Brompton Road
London SW3 2DY
+ 44 (0)20 7589 7001
Stylish children's clothing company, with enticing range of children's bedlinen, featuring duvet sets, cushions and quilts in soft colours.

Cath Kidston
www.cathkidston.co.uk
Duvet sets in nostalgic prints including classic cowboys and dinosaurs, jolly printed towels with ducks or stars, and co-ordinating wallpapers and floor tiles.

The Little White Company
www.thewhitecompany.com
0844 736 4222
Pretty bed linens and accessories for nursery, boys and girls in classic colours like red, blue and pink, plus timeless bedroom furniture in white.

FLOORING/TILES
Harvey Maria
www.harveymaria.co.uk
0845 6801231
Fabulous choice of practical, family-friendly flooring. Choose from plains in bright colours, Cath Kidston and Neisha Crosland designer ranges, and photo effect patterns.

The Rubber Flooring Company
www.therubberflooringcompany.co.uk
0800 849 6386
An extensive range of textured, tile effect and plain rubber flooring in neutral and bright colours.

ACCESSORIES
Bodie and Fou
www.bodieandfou.com
Exciting online store for design-conscious parents and kids, including wall stickers, funky animal lighting, and wallpapers.

Bombay Duck
www.bombayduck.com,
+ 44 (0)20 8749 3000
Sweet padded alphabet letters, wall hooks, storage, wall stickers and bunting for baby, boys and girls bedrooms.

Cox & Cox
www.coxandcox.co.uk
0844 858 0734
Beautiful homewares for all the family, with a big kids section, featuring inspired lighting, rugs, beanbags and wall art.

Not on the High Street
www.notonthehighstreet.com,
A broad range of kids' accessories from personalized cushions to kids' play tables and chairs, toy boxes and rugs.

White Rabbit England
www.whiterabbitengland.com
+ 44 (0)1625 419622
Traditional hand-painted earthenware toadstool nightlights and bone china lights in animal shapes, plus co-ordinating bedding and accessories.

USA

ONE-STOP STORES
Giggle
www.giggle.com
A chain of "new parent" stores offering a broad choice of modern cots, gliders, high chairs and fun kids furniture, all aimed at the stylish family home.

Mini Jake
www.minijake.com
178 N 9th St, Williamsbury
Brooklyn, New York
A modern children's store in Brooklyn with cool storage, kids' seating, children's beds and modern play furniture.

Pottery Barn Kids
www.potterybarnkids.com
The department store offers its own ranges of kids' furniture and accessories for nursery, girls and boys' bedrooms, work spaces and play rooms, plus co-ordinating ranges of bedding and bathroom accessories.

The Land of Nod
www.landofnod.com
Brilliant one-stop store offering children's bedroom furniture, nursery kit, colourful storage and accessories.

ONLINE STORES
Baby Bubble NYC
www.babybubblenyc.com
Online children's boutique offering chic kids' clothes plus a small but fun collection of homeware including cute mobiles, cushions and toys.

FURNITURE
Casa Kids
www.casakids.com
A smart, modern range of beds, playroom pieces and desks for kids featuring clean lines, designed by architect Roberto Gil.

Knoll Kids
www.knoll.com
The classic furniture company has a full range of scaled-down furniture for kids, including the Bertoia Diamond Chair and Saarinen's Womb Chair.

Oeuf
www.oeufnyc.com
High quality, multifunctional kids furniture designed by a French-American husband and wife team, with crisply styled modern pieces and organic layette collections.

BED LINEN
ABC Carpet and Home
www.abchome.com
New York's vast department store has a good baby and kids bedding section, offering everything from coloured organic cotton baby blankets to nursery patchwork quilts.

Dwell Studio
www.dwellstudio.com
Innovative, modern bed linens for kids, including butterfly, star and owl designs and nursery bedding sets, plus a whole range of furniture, wallpapers, and colourful rugs.

picture credits

All photographs by Debi Treloar unless otherwise stated.
Key: l left r right b below t top c centre

2 An apartment in London by Malin Iovino Design; 3 Vincent & Frieda Plasschaert's house in Brugge, Belgium; 5 The Boyes' home in London designed by Circus Architects; 12–13 Victoria Andreae's house in London; 14–15 Ab Rogers & Sophie Braimbridge's House, London, designed by Richard Rogers for his mother. Furniture design by KRD–Kitchen Rogers Design; 16–17 Sophie Eadie's house in London; 18–19 Rudi, Melissa & Archie Thackry's house in London; 20 c & l An apartment in London by Malin Iovino Design; 20 bl Designed by Sage and Coombe Architects, New York; 21 Vincent & Frieda Plasschaert's house in Brugge, Belgium; 24–25 Julia & David O'Driscoll's house in London; 26–27 Ben Johns & Deb Waterman Johns' house in Georgetown; 28–29 Michele Johnson's house in London designed by Nico Rensch Architeam; 30–31 The Zwirner's loft in New York; 34–35 Designed by Sage and Coombe Architects, New York; 36–37 The Boyes' home in London designed by Circus Architects; 38 Designed by Sage and Coombe Architects, New York; 42–47 Victoria Andreae's house in London; 48 Sera Hersham-Loftus' house in London; 50 l Suzanne & Christopher Sharp's house in London; 50 r– 51 The Zwirner's loft in New York; 53–55 Sudi Pigott's house in London; 56 Elizabeth Alford & Michael Young's loft in New York; 57 Sophie Eadie's house in London; 58–59 Julia & David O'Driscoll's house in London; 62– 65 Eben & Nica Cooper's bedroom, the Cooper family playroom; 67 Sue & Lars-Christian Brask's house in London designed by Susie Atkinson Design; 68–69 Pear Tree Cottage, Somerset, mural by Bruce Munro; 70–71 Suzanne & Christopher Sharp's house in London; 72 An apartment in New York designed by Steven Learner Studio; 73 Vincent & Frieda Plasschaert's house in Brugge, Belgium; 74–75 Ben Johns & Deb Waterman Johns' house in Georgetown; 78–79 Vincent & Frieda Plasschaert's house in Brugge, Belgium; 80 bl Sophie Eadie's house in London; 80 bc David & Macarena Wheldon's house in London designed by Fiona McLean; 80 br Sera Hersham-Loftus' house in London; 81 bl & br Ben Johns & Deb Waterman Johns' house in Georgetown; 84 l Ab Rogers & Sophie Braimbridge's House, London, designed by Richard Rogers for his mother. Furniture design by KRD–Kitchen Rogers Design; 84 br Designed by Ash Sakula Architects; 85 An apartment in New York designed by Steven Learner Studio; 86 Sudi Pigott's house in London; 87 Ben Johns & Deb Waterman Johns' house in Georgetown; 88–89 photographer Caroline Arber/Archie & Pink, London E1, loft designed by Will White; 90–91 David & Macarena Wheldon's house in London designed by Fiona McLean; 92–93 Vincent & Frieda Plasschaert's house in Brugge, Belgium; 94 tl Designed by Ash Sakula Architects; 94 b An apartment in London by Malin Iovino Design; 95 Ben Johns & Deb Waterman Johns' house in Georgetown; 96 main An apartment in London by Malin Iovino Design; 96 tcr, lc & lb Belén Moneo & Jeff Brock's apartment in New York designed by Moneo Brock Studio; 96 tr Ben Johns & Deb Waterman Johns' house in Georgetown; 97 main Elizabeth Alford & Michael Young's loft in New York; 97 tl & tr An apartment in London by Malin Iovino Design; 98–99 Hans & Lena Blomberg's house designed by Orefelt Associates; 100 tl An apartment in London by Malin Iovino Design; 100 tr Vincent & Frieda Plasschaert's house in Brugge, Belgium; 100 bl An apartment in New York designed by Steven Learner Studio; 100 bc Eben & Nica Cooper's bedroom, the Cooper family playroom; 100 br Ab Rogers & Sophie Braimbridge's House, London, designed by Richard Rogers for his mother. Furniture design by KRD–Kitchen Rogers Design; 102–103 The Zwirner's loft in New York; 106–107 Designed by Ash Sakula Architects; 108 l Victoria Andreae's house in London; 108 r Sophie Eadie's house in London; 109 l David & Macarena Wheldon's house in London designed by Fiona McLean; 109 r The Zwirner's loft in New York; 112 l Victoria Andreae's house in London; 112 r The Zwirner's loft in New York; 113 l & r Designed by Sage and Coombe Architects, New York; 116 & 117 b Belén Moneo & Jeff Brock's apartment in New York designed by Moneo Brock Studio; 117 t & c Designed by Ash Sakula; 120 David & Macarena Wheldon's house in London designed by Fiona McLean ; 121 Designed by Sage and Coombe Architects, New York; 122 t & 123 Victoria Andreae's house in London; 126–127 Michele Johnson's house in London designed by Nico Rensch Architeam; 128 Victoria Andreae's house in London; 129 t Charlotte Crosland's house in London; 129 b Ben Johns & Deb Waterman Johns' house in Georgetown; 130–131 playhouse by Dan Levy; 133 main & tc, cr, & br Sarah Gredley's house in London, tree house designed by Kim Woolfe-Murray; 134–135 Ben Johns & Deb Waterman Johns' house in Georgetown.

architects and designers

Elizabeth Alford Design
60 Thomas Street
New York, NY 10013
USA
t. 001 212 385 2185
f. 001 212 385 2186
e. esa799@banet.net
56; 97 main

Ash Sakula Architects
24 Rosebery Avenue
London EC1R 4SX
t. 020 7837 9735
www.ashsak.com
84 br; 94 tl; 106–107;
117 t & c

Circus Architects
1a Summer's Street
London EC1R 5BD
t. 020 7833 1999
f. 020 7833 1888
5; 36–37

Charlotte Crosland
Wingrave Crosland Interiors
t. 020 8960 9442
f. 020 8960 9714
129 t

Malin Iovino Design
t. 020 7252 3542
f. 020 7252 3542
e. iovino@btconnect.com
2; 20 c & l; 94 b; 96 main; 97
tl & tr; 100 tl

KRD–Kitchen Rogers Design
t. 020 8944 7088
e. ab@krd.demon.co.uk
14–15; 84 l; 100 br

Dan Levy
artist / woodworker
34 Summerfield Avenue
London NW6 6JY
t. 020 8969 8428
130–131

Fiona McLean
McLean Quinlan Architects
t. 020 8767 1633
80 bc; 90–91; 109 l; 120

Jeff Brock and Belén Moneo
Moneo Brock Studio
371 Broadway, 2nd floor
New York, NY 10013
USA
www.moneobrock.com
96 tcr, lc & lb; 116 & 117 tr

Bruce Munro
Mural commissions
t. 01749 813 898
f. 01749 813 515
e. brucemunro@freenet.co.uk
68–69

Nico Rensch Architeam
t. 01424 445885
www.architeam.co.uk
28–29; 126–127

Orefelt Associates
43 Pall Mall Deposit
124–128 Barlby Road
London W10 6BL
t. 020 8960 2560
98–99

Sage and Coombe Architects
205 Hudson Street
Suite 1002
New York, NY 10013
USA
t. 001 212 226 9600
f. 001 212 226 8456
www.sageandcoombe.com
20 r; 34–35; 38; 113 l
& r; 121

Susie Atkinson Design
t. 0468 814 134
67

Steven Learner Studio
307 Seventh Avenue
New York, NY 10001
USA
t. 001 212 741 8583
f. 001 212 741 2180
www.stevenlearnerstudio.com
72; 85; 100 bl

Kim Woolfe-Murray
Urban & Country Tree Houses
34 North Junction Road
Edinburgh EH6 6HP
t. 0131 553 5554
133 main, tc, cr & br

Will White Design
326 Portobello Road
London W10 5RU
t. 020 8964 8052
f. 020 8964 8050
e. willwhite.design@virgin.net
88–89

index

Page numbers in italics refer to captions.

acknowledgments

Thank you to Anne Ryland, whose eyes lit up, instead of glazed over, when I first mooted the idea of a *children's* contemporary decorating book.

A huge thank you to Debi Treloar, for her limitless energy, amazing patience with children and fabulous photographs. To Louise Leffler, for her deft creative vision; to Kate Brunt, for tremendous locations; and to Gabriella Le Grazie, for her watchful eye. Thank you Alison Starling and Annabel Morgan, for your spot-on editorial support.

Thank you to all the parents who so kindly welcomed us into their private family spaces, and to every child we photographed. It was a privilege to see your bedrooms, guys – I hope we didn't tidy up too much!

Thank you Anthony, Cicely and Felix. Our family life has been the inspiration for this book. And thank you to *my* parents, Harry and Ann, who when I was a child generously humoured my nascent decorating streak and let me design my bedroom at a very tender age.